CORYDON

CORYDON

by André Gide

With a comment on the second dialogue in CORYDON *by* FRANK BEACH, *Department of Psychology, Yale University.*

NOONDAY PRESS

a division of

FARRAR, STRAUS and GIROUX

CONTENTS

PUBLISHER'S NOTE

The reader's attention is directed to Dr. Frank Beach's "Comments on the Second Dialogue in *Corydon*," which follow the appendices in English translation. They are published as appendix rather than introduction so that the reader will be inclined to read the famous dialogue before the comment on it. Dr. Beach's research in psychology and biology is well known, and the comment, unsparing and illuminating as it is, is included with Mr. Gide's complete approval.

The history of the publication of the dialogues is as follows:

The first edition of *Corydon* consisted of only the first two dialogues and a short part of the third. It appeared under the title "C.R.D.N." without name of author, publisher, or place of publication, but with the imprint: Imprimerie Sainte-Catherine, Bruges, 22 May, 1911. Of this first edition André Gide refers (in his preface to the second edition) to 12 copies, whereas Arnold Naville in his Bibliography refers to 22 copies. In any case there were only a few and they were not for sale.

The second edition in 1920, consisting of 21 copies, was again not for sale. It appeared under the title *Corydon*, but was still without name of author, publisher, or place of publication, but with the imprint: Imprimerie Sainte-Catherine, Bruges, 5 May, 1920. This second edition consisted of Four Socratic Dialogues and a Preface.

The first published edition was that of the *Nouvelle Revue Française* in 1924, under the title *Corydon* and with the name of the author. There were 550 copies on Holland and 5,000 on ordinary paper. Although the copies on Holland were dated 7 January, 1924, and those on ordinary paper 9 January, 1924, the edition was not on sale until May, 1924.

Reprints have since followed. The current edition is numbered the 66th, representing some 33,000 copies.

Hitherto there have been only the following translations of *Corydon*:

1) A German translation by Joachim Moras was published in the *Deutsche Verlag Anstalt* in 1932.

2) The contract for a Spanish translation was arranged and signed with the Spanish publisher Ruiz Castillo in 1925. While there is no available evidence that this translation did appear, there is no reason to believe that it did not.

3) An Italian translation to be published by Mondadori is in course of preparation.

PREFACE TO
THE FIRST EDITION
IN ENGLISH

A Swedish interviewer came to Neuchâtel, where I was recovering from a heart attack. Ordinarily I do not give interviews, but I had just received the Nobel Prize, and as this journalist was correspondent for the X—— of Stockholm, I could not decently refuse him. Moreover he was charming and I retain a most pleasant memory of the conversation that I had with him. Before leaving, he asked me whether there was not one book that I regretted having written. Was he referring to my *Back from the U.S.S.R.?* I looked at him, and since in asking the question, he endeavored to smile tactfully, I realized that he must be referring to *Corydon.* I replied, without smiling, that I would certainly have renounced the Nobel Prize rather than retract any single one of my writings. No title, however, had yet been mentioned; but when the interviewer asked me, immediately afterwards, which of my books I considered the most important, without a moment's hesitation I named *Corydon*. I begged him all the same not to overstress this pronouncement, which ran the risk of appearing paradoxical (I do not like paradoxes) and of assuming an air of defiance, extremely uncivil to the friends I might have in Sweden. The Nobel Prize had been awarded me *in spite of* this book, which in itself should have been enough for me. It would have been discourteous and arrogant for me to have overemphasized a point which others perhaps endeavored to forget.

Corydon remains in my opinion the most important of my books; but it is also the one with which I find most fault. The least successful is the very one which should have been the most successful. No doubt I was ill-advised to treat ironically questions of such gravity, which are usually only regarded as subjects for censure or ridicule. If I returned to these questions, then it would certainly be thought that I was obsessed by them. People prefer to pass them over in silence, as though they played but a negligible rôle in society, and as though the number of people in society tormented by these questions was negligible too. And yet when I began to write my book, I believed this number to be far smaller than I have subsequently come to realize and than is actually the case; smaller perhaps in France, however, than in many other countries that I came to learn about later; for in no other country (except Spain) have the cult of woman, the religion of love and a certain tradition of dalliance so subjugated convention or so slavishly prescribed the conduct of life. Clearly I am not referring here to the cult of woman in the form which commands the deepest respect, nor to love in its noblest sense, but to that love which degrades and which sacrifices to the wanton bed and bawd all that is best in man. Those who shrug their shoulders at these questions are the very ones who proclaim that love is the most important thing in life, and who find it quite natural that men should subordinate their careers to it. For them this is, of course, a matter of sexual desire and satisfaction, and in their view desire is the supreme authority. But according to them this desire loses all value when it fails to conform with their own. They are very confident in their attitude, having public opinion behind them.

I believe however that in this book I have said almost all that I had to say on this extremely important subject that had not been said before; and I am convinced also that the day will come when its importance will be recognized. In France it has been kept hidden under a bushel, and I am rather relying on the fact that in America it will emerge from this obscurity, to which I myself deliberately relegated it, as a precaution against unnecessary scandal. It has been said that love of scandal drove me to write it. On the contrary, I have done everything possible to mitigate the scandal which this book might provoke, even so far as its form is concerned: for if I had to rewrite it today, I would do so in a far more affirmative tone and no longer with any irony; partly because my voice has assumed more assurance, and partly because I have come to realize that I was far more in the right than at first I dared to believe. I knew that the book could wait. Its hour, in France at least, has not yet arrived. In America perhaps it has? The publication and circulation of the *Kinsey Report* allows me to suppose and hope so.

I do not attempt to delude myself as to the inadequacies and imperfections of this book. But such as it is (and I cannot rewrite it), I shall be satisfied if it helps a little to tear down or lift the thick veil of lies, conventions and hypocrisy which still stifles an important and not contemptible part of humanity.

PREFACE TO
THE THIRD FRENCH EDITION

My friends insist that this is the kind of book that will do me the greatest harm. I do not believe it will rob me of anything I value; or rather, I do not attach much importance to those things it can deprive me of: acclaim, decorations, honors, the entrée into fashionable society, in fact all the things I have never sought. I only value the esteem of a few rare spirits who will, I hope, understand that my greatest merit lies in having written this book and in daring to publish it today. I hope not to lose this esteem; but I would certainly rather lose it than feel that I owed it to any deception or misunderstanding.

I have never attempted to please the public; but I do attach enormous importance to the opinion of a few. It is a matter of sentiment and nothing can alter it. What has sometimes been taken for a kind of intellectual timidity on my part was usually nothing but the fear of hurting these people; and of hurting one person in particular who has always been dear to me above all others. Who can say how many hesitations, reticences and digressions are due to consideration and affection? As for simple delays, I cannot hold them regrettable, believing as I do that artists of our time err most often through a great lack of patience. Many of the works served up to us today would have been improved had they been given the opportunity to mature. Ideas which at first appear brilliant may perish tomorrow. For this reason I waited a long time to write this book, and, once it was written, to publish it. I wanted to be certain that I would not have to retract what I had written in *Corydon* and which seemed to me so self-evident. But no! my ideas have been confirmed by time, and the only reproach I have against myself is that this book should be so reserved and timid. The ten years which have elapsed since it was written have brought fresh examples, arguments and evidence to corroborate my theories. What I believed before the war, I believe more strongly today. The indignation that *Corydon* will arouse does not shake my belief that what I say here ought to be said. Not that I consider one should say all one thinks, and say it whenever one chooses—but this must be said, and now is the time.[1]

Certain friends to whom I first submitted the book considered that I paid too much attention to questions of natural history—whilst I was not wrong in attaching so much importance to them, they thought these questions would tire and deter the reader. Splendid! That is just what I hope. I have not written to amuse and I must immediately undeceive anyone who is looking for entertainment, wit, artistic achievement or anything else but the simplest expression of a very serious theme.

Finally, I certainly do not believe that wisdom consists of abandoning oneself to one's natural instincts and giving them free rein; but I do believe that, before attempting to subdue and tame them, it is essential to understand them fully—for a number of the discords we have to endure are unwarranted and are due entirely to errors of interpretation.

November, 1922

PREFACE TO
THE SECOND FRENCH EDITION

After waiting eight years, I have decided to re-print this short book. It first appeared in 1911, in an edition of twelve copies, all of which have been put away in a drawer, from which they have never been taken.

At that time *Corydon* consisted only of the first two dialogues and part of the third. The rest of the book was only sketched. Friends dissuaded me from completing it. "Friends," said Ibsen, "are dangerous, not so much for what they make one do, but for what they prevent one from doing." However, the views I developed in this book seemed to me of the greatest importance and I considered it necessary to advance them. But, on the other hand, I felt deep concern for the public welfare, and was prepared to withhold my views if I thought that they would be too disturbing.

It was for this reason, rather than for personal considerations of discretion, that I locked *Corydon* away in a drawer and kept it there so long. Nevertheless, during the last few months I have persuaded myself that this book, however subversive it may seem, is directed only against falsehood, and that nothing is more unhealthy for an individual or society than the accredited falsehood.

For after all, I thought, what I say about the subject here is not a matter of supposition. It is a matter of fact. I try to explain the facts as they are. And since people do not usually want to admit the existence of these facts, I have examined or tried to examine them, with a view to determining whether they are really as deplorable as people suppose them to be.

1920

FIRST DIALOGUE

I

A sensational trial in the year 19—— brought up once again the complicated and troublesome question of homosexuality. For a short while it was the sole topic of conversation. I grew tired of listening to the theories and observations of ignorant, bigoted fools, and I wanted to clarify my own ideas. Realizing that the right to condemn or condone lay with reason and not with sentiment, I decided to go and interview Corydon. I had heard that he did not protest against certain unnatural tendencies, of which he was accused. I wanted to learn the right of the case and find what he had to say in justification.

It was ten years since I had last seen Corydon. At that time he was a high-spirited boy, generous, friendly, gentle and proud, whose bearing even then commanded a certain respect. He had been a brilliant medical student and his early work had won high approval in professional circles. After leaving the Lycée where we had been fellow students, we continued a long time to be fairly close friends. Then we were separated by several years of travel and when I returned to live in Paris, the reputation which his habits were beginning to earn him kept me from seeing him.

On entering his apartment I had none of the unpleasant impressions I feared I must expect. At the same time Corydon's own appearance was most correct, with even a trace of studied austerity. I searched his room in vain for those unmistakable signs of effeminacy, which experts claim they invariably discern in everything connected with homosexuals. However I did notice, over the mahogany desk, a large photographic copy of Michelangelo's "Creation of Man"—in which Adam is depicted lying naked on the primeval slime, his hand stretched in obedience to God's finger and his eyes raised in dazzled recognition of His presence. Corydon's professed interest in works of art would have sheltered him, had I expressed any surprise at the special subject he had chosen. On his work table stood the portrait of an old man with a long white beard, which I immediately recognized as the American, Walt Whitman, because it had appeared at the beginning of his translated works, which had just been produced by M. Bazalgette. M. Bazalgette had also published a biography of the poet, which I had recently come across and which I now used as a gambit for opening the discussion.

I

After reading Bazalgette's book, I can see no good reason why this portrait should be on display."

My remark was impertinent. Corydon pretended not to understand, but I insisted.

"One still has to admire Whitman's work," he replied, "however one chooses to interpret his morals . . ."

"You must admit however that your admiration for Whitman has somewhat diminished, since Bazalgette showed that his morals were not such as you had previously been pleased to ascribe to him."

"Your friend Bazalgette has shown absolutely nothing. All his reasoning depends on a syllogism, which can equally well be reversed:

"As his major premise, he states that homosexuality is an unnatural tendency.

"But Whitman was in perfect health. He was, properly speaking, the most perfect example presented in literature of the natural man . . ."

"*Therefore* Whitman was not a homosexual. That seems to me an inescapable conclusion."

"But there are sections of his work, where Bazalgette vainly attempts to translate the word 'love' by '*amitié*' or '*affection*' and 'sweet' by '*pur*,' since Whitman is addressing a 'comrade' . . . Yet the fact nevertheless remains that all the passionate, sensual, tender and fervent passages of his poems belong to the same order; that order which you call unnatural."

"I do not call it an 'order' at all. . . . But let's hear your own syllogism."

"Here it is:

"Whitman can be taken as an example of the normal man.

"*But* Whitman was a homosexual."

"*Therefore* homosexuality is normal. Splendid! Now it only remains to prove that Whitman was a homosexual. But since it's a question of begging the question, I still prefer Bazalgette's syllogism. It conflicts with common sense."

"The essential thing is not to avoid conflicting with common sense, but to avoid warring with the truth. I am preparing an article on Whitman; an answer to Bazalgette's arguments." [1]

"You devote a lot of attention to these questions of morals?"

"Yes, quite a lot, I admit. I am even preparing a fairly important study on the subject."

"Aren't the works of Moll, Krafft-Ebing and Raffalovitch enough for you?"

"They are not satisfactory. I would like to approach it differently."

"I have always thought it best to refer to these things as little as possible, and that often they only exist because some clumsy person discloses them. Furthermore, it is in bad taste to speak of them, because there will always be some good-for-nothing, who wants to practice precisely those things of which he pretends to disapprove."

"I do not pretend to disapprove."

"There is a rumor that you pose as being tolerant."

"You simply do not understand me. I see I must tell you the title of my work."

"Please do."

"I am writing a *Defense of Homosexuality*."

"Why not a *Eulogy*, while you are about it?"

"Because such a title would force my ideas. I am

afraid that some people will find even the word '*Defense*' too provocative."

"And will you dare publish it?"

"No," he said gravely, "I will not."

"You are all exactly the same," I continued after a short pause. "Alone amongst yourselves, you are defiantly confident; but out in the open, or faced with others, your courage evaporates. Deep down you know quite well that the censure heaped on you is perfectly justified. You protest eloquently in low voices, but when it comes to speaking up, you shirk it."

"It is true that the cause lacks martyrs."

"Don't use such big words."

"I use the words needed. We have had Wilde, Krupp, Macdonald, Eulenburg . . ."

"As if that were not enough for you!"

"Oh, victims! Victims as many as you please. But not a single martyr. They all deny it; they always will deny it."

"There you are! They all feel ashamed and retract as soon as they are faced with public opinion, the press or the courtroom."

"Or, alas! commit suicide. Yes, you are right. To try and establish one's innocence by disavowing one's life, is to yield to public opinion. How strange! One

9

has the courage of one's opinions, but not of one's habits. One can accept suffering, but not dishonor."

"By withholding publication of your book, aren't you the same as the others?"

He hesitated a moment, and then said, "Perhaps I shall not withhold it."

"Can you conceive what your attitude would be if, in court, you were cornered by a Queensberry or a Harden?"

"Yes, unfortunately! Like those before me, I should be put out of countenance and deny everything. Our lives are never so isolated that the mud flung at us will not, at the same time, spatter others who are dear to us. The scandal would break my mother's heart; I would never forgive myself. My young sister lives with her and is not yet married. Perhaps it would be hard to find someone who would accept me as his brother-in-law."

"Ah! I catch your meaning. You are admitting that these habits bring disgrace even to those who do no more than tolerate them."

"It is not an admission; it is a statement. And that is exactly why I think the cause needs martyrs."

"What do you mean by martyr?"

"Someone who would lead the attack; who would accept, without bluster or boasting, all the odium and insults; or better still, someone whose courage, integrity and uprightness were so incontestable that the most confirmed denouncers would hesitate."

"You will never find such a man."

"Let us hope he will appear."

"Listen! Between ourselves, do you think there would be the slightest use in it? What change of opinion can you expect? You, I admit, are fairly restrained. But, believe me, it would be better if you were even more so. These appalling habits would then quite naturally cease and would not reappear again."

I noticed him shrug his shoulders, but that did not deter me from continuing.

"Don't you think there is enough wickedness already exhibited in the world? I have been told that homosexuals find here and there shameful facilities; that they derive satisfaction from these hidden facilities and from the compliance of other homosexuals. Don't try to solicit the approval or even the indulgence of honest people on their behalf."

"It is precisely the esteem of honest people that I cannot afford to overlook."

"What can you do about it? Change your habits."

"I cannot change them. That was the dilemma

of Krupp, Macdonald and many others, and the revolver was their only solution."

"Luckily you are less tragic."

"I could not swear to that. Anyway, I would like to write my book."

"You must admit there is a certain element of conceit in your attitude."

"None at all."

"You cultivate your eccentricities, and then, to avoid any feeling of guilt, you congratulate yourself that you are different from the rest."

Once again he shrugged his shoulders, and paced the room without saying a word. Then, having apparently overcome the impatience which my last words aroused, he continued.

II

Not long ago," he said, sitting down beside me, "we were good friends, and knew how to understand one another. Is it really necessary for you now to retort ironically to everything I say? I am not asking for your approval, but, since I am speaking in good faith, could you not listen in good faith—then I could at least feel that you were listening to me in the same spirit that I was talking to you?"

"Forgive me," I said, disarmed by his tone of voice. "It is true that I have lost touch with you. Yes, we were fairly close friends before your behavior was affected by your inclinations."

"Then you stopped seeing me; or, to be honest, you broke with me."

"Let's not look for explanations. Let's talk as we used to," I said, holding out my hand. "I have time to listen. When we knew each other, you were still a student. Did you already understand yourself then? Tell me. I want to know the truth."

He turned to me with a new expression of confidence, and began:

"During my time as a house surgeon at the hospital, I was plunged into a state of the greatest confusion when I came to realize my . . . anomaly. It is absurd to maintain, as some people still do, that homosexuality is only the result of dissipation or that it is simply an addiction of the blasé. I could not see myself as either degenerate or sick. Hard-working and completely chaste, I lived with the firm intention, when I finished my time in hospital, of marrying a girl, since dead, whom I then loved above all else in the world.

"My love was too great for me to realize clearly that I had no physical desire for her. There are people, I know, who maintain that the one can exist without the other, but this did not occur to me. Moreover I had never loved any other woman, either spiritually or physically. The prostitutes, whom most of my friends pursued, were even less of a temptation to me. But since, at that time, I scarcely suspected that I might find attraction elsewhere, or that genuine attraction could even exist elsewhere, I persuaded myself that my abstention was a virtue; I prided myself on the idea of remaining a virgin until

14

marriage; I idealized the purity that I was unable to think of as a delusion. It was only slowly that I came to understand myself; and finally I had to admit that the temptations which I flattered myself on resisting had really no attraction for me.

"What I had held to be virtue was really nothing but indifference. This was an appallingly humiliating fact for a young and high-minded person to accept. Only by hard work did I succeed in overcoming the melancholy which darkened and discolored my life. I soon persuaded myself that I was unsuited for marriage and being unable to tell my fiancée the reasons for my sadness, my attitude towards her became more and more equivocal and embarrassed. Furthermore, the experiences that I then decided to try in a brothel proved to me conclusively that I was not impotent; while at the same time they served finally to convince me . . ."

"Convince you of what?"

"My case seemed so extraordinary (for how was I to know that it was common?). I saw myself capable of sexual activity; but I believed I was incapable of, so to speak, sexual desire. Born of extremely healthy parents, I was physically robust. My appearance did nothing to betray my misery. None of my friends suspected it. I would rather have died than let anyone know. But this farce of cheerfulness, which I felt obliged to play in order to avoid suspicion, became eventually unbearable. As soon as I was alone, I relapsed into despondency."

I was deeply impressed by the seriousness and conviction in his voice.

"You read too much into this," I said quietly. "You were simply in love, and therefore full of anxieties. Your love would have developed quite naturally into physical desire, as soon as you were married."

"I know people say so . . . but how right I was to be skeptical!"

"There is little trace of the hypochondriac about you now. How did you cure yourself?"

"At that time I was reading a lot, and in the course of my reading I came across a sentence which gave me some sound advice. It was from the abbé Galiani. 'The important thing,' he wrote to Mme. d'Épinay, 'the important thing is not so much to be cured, as to learn to live with one's sickness.' "

"Why don't you tell that to your patients?"

"I do, to those who are incurable. No doubt these words seem simple enough to you, but I drew my whole philosophy from them. It only remained for me to realize that I was not a freak, a unique case, for me to recover my self-assurance and escape from my self-hatred."

"You have explained how you came to realize your lack of interest in women, but not how your other inclinations . . ."

"That is a rather painful story and I do not like to tell it. However I think you will listen sympathetically, and perhaps the story will help you to treat these matters less lightly."

I reassured him, if not of my sympathy, then at least of my respectful attention.

"You already know," he began, "that I was engaged. I loved the girl whom I intended to marry tenderly, but with a love that was almost mystical, and naturally, with my lack of experience, I scarcely imagined that any other kind of real love could exist. My fiancée had a brother, a few years younger, whom I often saw and who formed a strong affection for me."

"Aha!" I exclaimed involuntarily.

Corydon looked up sharply.

"No! Nothing improper took place between us. His sister was my fiancée."

"Forgive me."

"But you can imagine my consternation, when one evening we were talking and he made it quite apparent that he wanted more than my friendship."

"Like most children, surely? They all require

17

a little tenderness. But it is up to us, who are older, to respect that."

"I can assure you that I did respect it. However, Alexis was no longer a child. He was an intelligent and perceptive boy. But what was doubly disconcerting for me was that he showed such extraordinary and precocious insight in describing his own feelings that I felt he was making my own confession. Nothing, however, could possibly justify my severity."

"Severity?"

"Yes! I was thoroughly scared. I spoke severely, almost harshly, and what was even worse, I spoke with the greatest contempt for what I called his effeminacy, which was in fact nothing but the natural expression of his affection."

"It is as well to handle such cases with delicacy."

"I used so little delicacy that the poor child—yes, he was only a kid—took my words tragically to heart. For three days he strove, by redoubled efforts of friendliness, to overcome what he took to be my anger; but I exaggerated my coldness towards him, to such an extent that . . ."

"Yes?"

"What! Don't you know that Alexis B. killed himself?"

"Are you trying to suggest that . . ."

"Oh! I am suggesting nothing. At first they spoke of an accident. We were in the country at the time. The body was found at the foot of a cliff. An accident? What was I to believe? But here is the letter which I found on my bed."

He opened a drawer with an unsteady hand, glanced at the letter and then said:

"No, I shall not read it to you. You would misjudge the boy. He told me in the most moving terms of the agony into which he had been thrown by our last conversation—particularly certain of my expressions. 'You can only save yourself from this,' I had cried, hypocritically indignant at the feelings he had confessed to me, 'you can only be saved by means of a great love.' 'Alas,' he wrote, 'I feel that love for you, my friend. You have not understood me; or, what is worse, you have understood and have despised me for it. I see I am becoming an object of disgust to you, as indeed I am becoming to myself. If I cannot change my awful nature, I can at least suppress it . . .' Then four more pages of pathetic writing, which on account of his age was a little pompous and which afterwards it is so easy to belittle as simply declamatory."

This speech made me feel a little uncomfortable . . .

"It was obviously," I said at last, "a malicious trick of fate for such a declaration of love to be addressed to you in particular; and I can well understand how the episode must have upset you."

"To such an extent that I immediately gave up all thought of marrying my friend's sister."

"But," I persisted, "I am convinced that people only get what they deserve. You must admit that if this boy had not sensed in you some possible echo of his own guilty passion, then his passion . . ."

"Perhaps some obscure instinct did make him aware of it; but in that case it was a pity that it did not make me aware of it too."

"If you had been aware of it, what would you have done?"

"I believe I would have cured the boy."

"You said a moment ago that it was incurable. You quoted the words of the abbé. 'The important thing is not so much to be cured . . .'"

"I could have cured him, as I have cured myself."

"And how is that?"

"By persuading him he was not sick."

"Now tell me his perversion was natural!"

". . . By persuading him that there was nothing unnatural in his deviation."

"And if it had persisted, you would naturally have yielded to it."

"Ah! that is an entirely different question. When the physiological problem is resolved, the moral problem begins. Out of consideration for his sister, I would certainly have urged him to conquer his feelings, in the same way that I would have conquered my own. At least his love would have lost the monstrous appearance which it had assumed in his eyes.
. . . This drama, by opening my own eyes to my true character and by showing me the nature of my affection for this boy; this drama, on which I meditated so long, finally determined my attitude towards . . . the thing which you find so despicable. Remembering this victim, I wanted to help other victims suffering from the same misunderstanding. I wanted to cure them in the way that I have told you."

III

Now I think you will appreciate why I want to write this book. The only serious books on the subject, to my knowledge, are certain medical works, which from the opening pages reek unbearably of the clinic . . ."

"Then you do not intend to write as a doctor?"

"As doctor, naturalist, moralist, sociologist, historian . . ."

"I was not aware you were so versatile."

"What I mean to say is that I shall not claim to write about it as a specialist, but as a man. Usually the doctors who deal with the subject are only concerned with homosexuals who feel ashamed; the pitiful, the plaintive, the inverted, the sick. Only these resort to doctors. As a doctor myself, I have to attend such people; but as a man I come across others who are neither pitiful nor complaining—it is these that I wish to study."

"The normal homosexuals!"

"Exactly. You must understand that in homosexuality as in heterosexuality, there are all shades and degrees: from Platonic love to lust, from self-denial to sadism, from healthy joy to moroseness, from natural development to all the refinements of vice. And between exclusive homosexuality and exclusive heterosexuality there is every intermediate shade. It is usual, however, to make a clear-cut distinction between normal love and love which is allegedly unnatural—and, for convenience, to attribute to the one all the happiness, all the noble and tragic passions, all the splendor of spirit, and all heroic achievement; whilst loading on the other all the foul dregs of . . ."

"Don't let yourself get carried away. Sapphism is not altogether unrecognized amongst us."

He was so worked up that he did not hear my remark and continued:

"There is no spectacle more grotesque, at each new trial for a moral offense, than the righteous astonishment of the newspapers at the virile appearance of the accused. Evidently the public expected to see them in skirts. Look! I cut this out of the *Journal* at the time of the Harden trial."

23

He searched amongst some documents and handed me a sheet of paper where the following was underlined:

The Count de Hohenau, tall, well dressed and dignified, does not give the slightest impression of being an effeminate man. He is the typical example of the Guards officer, proud of his profession. And yet this man, with his splendid military appearance, is suspected of the gravest offense. The Count de Lynar, a handsome man also . . . etc.

"In the same way," he continued, "Macdonald and Eulenburg seemed, even to the most prejudiced observers, intelligent, handsome, dignified . . ."

"In fact very attractive men!"

He stopped for a moment and I noticed a look of scorn on his face. But recovering quickly, he continued as though he had not caught my meaning:

"One could rightly expect the person loved to be attractive, but not necessarily the person who loves. The appearance of these people does not affect me. If I insist on physical appearances, then it is only because of the significant fact that they are healthy and virile. I do not claim that all homosexuals are. Homosexuality, like heterosexuality, has its degenerates, its vicious and its sick. Like most of my

24

fellow doctors, I have come across many pitiful, painful and dubious cases. But I will spare my readers. As I have said already, my book will deal with healthy homosexuality, or as you expressed it just now, with 'normal homosexuality.' "

"Didn't you realize that I was using the phrase mockingly? You would be delighted if I had to concede this first point."

"I shall never ask you to concede anything out of kindness. I would rather you were forced to do so."

"Now it is your turn to joke."

"I am not joking. I don't mind betting that within twenty years it will be impossible to take words like 'unnatural' and 'perverted' at all seriously. There is only one thing in the world that I admit is not natural: a work of art. Everything else, whether one likes it or not, belongs to the natural order, and since we are no longer regarding it from a moralist's point of view, it is best to consider it from a naturalist's."

"These words that you are challenging are at least useful in strengthening our moral customs. Where should we be if you were to eliminate them?"

"We should not be more amoral; in fact I have to restrain myself from adding, 'on the contrary!' . . . You heterosexuals are magnificent humbugs. Listening to some of you talk one would gather that for a relationship to be licit or at any rate 'normal,' it is only necessary for it to be between people of different sexes."

"It is sufficient if the relationship is potentially normal. But homosexuals are of necessity depraved."

"Do you really imagine that they know nothing of self-control and self-denial?"

"It is, of course, lucky that they are restrained to some extent by our laws and by a certain sense of respectability."

"And it is, of course, lucky for you that our laws and conventions restrain you so little."

"I am losing my patience! We have marriage, good honest marriage, which is more than you have. You make me feel like one of those moralists who regard all pleasures of the flesh as sinful, except those of marriage and who disapprove of any relationship that is not legally sanctioned."

"Oh! I can tell them a thing or two about that; and, if driven to it, can be as uncompromising as they are. I have been called on, as a doctor, to probe into a considerable number of marital relationships, very few of which, I can assure you, were spotless, and I would certainly not like to wager that more ingenuity in the mechanics of love (or perversions if you prefer) is to be found amongst professional prostitutes than amongst certain 'honest' couples."

"You are revolting."

"But if the bed is a marriage bed, then vice is immediately whitewashed."

"Married couples can do what they like. That is permissible. Anyway it is none of your business."

" 'Permissible'; yes, I prefer that word to 'normal.' "

"I had been warned that you people possessed a strangely distorted moral sense. But I had no idea it was as bad as this! You seem to be overlooking completely the natural act of procreation which marriage sanctifies and by which the great mystery of life is perpetuated."

"And once that is achieved, the act of love becomes an unlicensed intoxication, nothing but a gratuitous fantasy, a game. Ah no! I am not overlooking it. In fact I intend to base my theories on its inescapable conclusions. Apart from the demands of procreation, there remains nothing but the pleasure principle. But remember that the act of procreation is rare and that once every ten months is sufficient."

"That is very little."

"Very little; especially when the natural urge requires an infinitely greater outlet, and . . . I hardly dare finish my sentence."

"Go on. You have said so much already."

"All right then. I maintain that the act of procreation in Nature, so far from being the only 'natural' factor, is, to a disconcerting degree, usually nothing but a fluke."

"Good God! Explain yourself."

"Willingly. But at this point we come to natural history, with which my book begins and from which I approach my subject. If you have the patience, I shall explain it to you. Come back tomorrow. By then I shall have put my papers in order."

SECOND DIALOGUE

The following day, at about the same time, I returned to Corydon's apartment.

"I nearly decided not to come back," I said on entering.

"I knew you would say that," he answered, as he invited me to sit down, "but that nevertheless you would come back."

"That was shrewd of you. But if you don't mind, today I have come to listen to a naturalist and not a psychologist."

"Don't worry. I am prepared to speak about natural history. My notes are arranged and if I chose to use them all, I should require at least three volumes. But, as I told you yesterday, I am deliberately discarding all medical material; not because it holds no interest for me, but because I shall not require it till later. In my book there is no need for it."

"You speak as though it were already written."

"It is at least prepared; but there is such a quantity of material that I have divided it into three parts."

"And the first will consist of natural history."

"Which will last us for today."

"May I ask what will be included in the second?"

"If you return tomorrow, we will discuss history, literature and the arts."

"And the day after tomorrow?"

"I shall do my best to satisfy you from the point of view of sociology and morality."

"And after that?"

"After that I shall say goodbye and let others have their say."

"In the meantime I want to hear what you have to say. So begin."

I

I am taking certain precautions in broaching my subject and intend to quote from Pascal and Montaigne."

"What light do they have to throw on it?"

"Listen. Here are two quotations that I want to select and emphasize. They seem to me to set the discussion on the proper footing."

"Let's hear the quotations."

"You know this one from Pascal: *I am very much afraid that this so-called nature may itself be no more than an early custom, just as custom is second nature.*"

"Yes, I must have seen it."

"I emphasize: '*I am very much afraid . . .*'"

"Why?"

"Because I am glad he should be afraid. There must be something in it."

"And the Montaigne?"

"*The laws of conscience, which we say have their origins in Nature, originate in custom.*"

"I know that you are well read. One can find what one wants in a good library by thorough searching. Of course it does not matter at all picking a random line from Pascal, interpreting it as you please and then having the nerve to shelter behind him."

"Do you imagine that there were not plenty of others to choose from? I have copied a number of his sayings which show that I have not misrepresented his ideas. Read these."

He handed me a sheet of paper on which the following words were copied: *Man's nature is completely natural,* omne animal. *Nothing can be made natural. Nothing natural can be made to lose its nature.*

"Or if you prefer . . ."

He handed me another sheet of paper on which I read: *Undoubtedly Nature is not altogether uniform. It is custom that produces this, for it constrains Nature. But sometimes Nature overcomes it, and confines man to his instinct, despite every custom, good or bad.*

"Are you claiming that heterosexuality is simply a matter of custom?"

"Not at all. But that we are judging according to custom when we maintain that only heterosexuality is natural."

"Pascal would be flattered if he knew the use to which you were putting him."

"I don't think I am distorting his ideas. The important thing to understand is that when you say 'unnatural,' the word 'uncustomary' would be sufficient. Once convinced of that, we can approach the question with less prejudice, I hope."

"Your quotation is double-edged, and I can turn it against you. Homosexual habits, imported into Europe from Asia or Africa, and into France from Germany, England or Italy, have occasionally, here and there, been able to contaminate us. But, thank God, the natural, healthy instincts of good old France have always prevailed; fundamentally decent, as one would expect." [1]

Corydon rose and paced the room for a few moments in silence. Then he continued:

"I must beg you, my dear friend, not to drag questions of nationalism into the discussion. In Africa, where I have traveled, the Europeans are convinced that this practice is the accepted thing. Acting on this assumption and encouraged by the beauty of the people, they indulge it more freely than they would do in their own country; with the result that the Mussulmen, for their part, are convinced that these habits come from Europe."

"Anyway I believe that example and influence

play some part; that the laws of imitation . . ."

"But surely you realize that they operate just as well in the opposite direction? Do you remember de La Rochefoucauld's profound words: *There are people who would never have loved, if they had not heard others speak of love?* Think how everything in our society and our customs directs one sex towards the other. Everything teaches heterosexuality. Everything evokes and encourages it; books, theatres, magazines, the example set by older people, the whole parade of drawing room and gutter. *If one does not fall in love as a result of all this, one has been badly brought up*, the younger Dumas humorously remarked in the preface to *The Question of Money*. Yet if the adolescent finally succumbs to this powerful conspiracy, then you are not willing to admit that any influence guided his choice or that pressure molded his desires into the approved form. But if on the other hand, in spite of all this advice, encouragement and provocation, he displays a tendency towards homosexuality, then immediately you lay the blame on reading or some other influence (and you argue in the same way for an entire nation); you assert that it is an acquired taste; he must surely have been taught it. You refuse to admit that he can have discovered it for himself."

"I do not admit that he could have discovered it,

if he were healthy; simply because I do not recognize this as a spontaneous taste, except in people who are inverted, degenerate or sick."

"But really! Here you have this taste, this propensity, which everything tries to conceal and thwart, which is not permitted to appear in art, in books or in life; which, if it does appear, falls immediately under the axe of the Law and is exposed in the pillory of public disgrace, a butt for cheap jokes, insults and almost universal contempt . . ."

"Keep calm! Keep calm! Your homosexual is a great discoverer."

"I do not say that he always discovers it for himself; but I do say that when he is following someone else's example, then it is because he wishes to follow it and because that example has fostered his secret inclinations."

"You certainly cling to your contention that the inclination is innate."

"I simply state it as a fact . . . and perhaps you will allow me to point out that this inclination can hardly be inherited, for the specious reason that the act, by which it could be transmitted, is necessarily a heterosexual act . . ."

"An ingenious conceit!"

"You have to admit, however, that this instinct must be irrepressibly strong, deeply ingrained in the flesh itself, or to use the word again, it must be profoundly *natural* to withstand so much abuse and utterly refuse to disappear. It resembles, don't you think, an ever-flowing spring which one assiduously tries to stem, only to find it breaking out again further on, since it is impossible to quench the source. Rage to your heart's content! Repress! Oppress! You will never suppress it!"

"I agree that the cases reported in the press have become deplorably frequent in recent years."

"That is because the newspapers, as a result of certain celebrated cases, have acquired the habit of reporting on it. The apparent frequency of homosexuality depends on how openly it flourishes. The truth of the matter is that this instinct, which you call unnatural, has always existed to about the same extent in all places and at all times—like every other natural appetite."

"What was Pascal's phrase: *All tastes are to be found in Nature . . . ?*"

"*No doubt Nature is not so uniform. It is therefore custom which causes this by constraining Nature; and sometimes Nature surmounts it and keeps man within the bounds of instinct . . .*"

"I am beginning to understand you better. But at that rate you will have to maintain that sadism,

murder and all the lowest instincts are equally natural . . . and that will not have got you far."

"I do in fact believe that no instinct exists for
which authority cannot be found in some animal
habit. Cats are unable to feel any excitement unless
their love-making is accompanied by biting. . . .
But we are digressing. . . . I believe furthermore,
and for reasons which are fairly easy to appreciate,
that sadism more readily accompanies heterosexuality than homosexuality. Let us say, for simplicity's
sake if you like, that there are social and anti-social
instincts. Whether or not homosexuality is an anti-
social instinct, I shall examine in the second and
third parts of my book; so for the moment let me
defer the question. I have first of all not only to establish that homosexuality is natural, but also to try
and give a reasonable explanation for its existence.
Perhaps these preliminary remarks will not have
been altogether out of place, since I must tell you
that what I am about to formulate is nothing less
than a new theory of love."

"Damn it! Is the old theory not good enough for
you?"

"Apparently not, since its result is to make homosexuality an unnatural business. We live steeped
in a very old and very ordinary theory of love, which

39

we no longer think of discussing; a theory that has penetrated deep into natural history, biasing a great deal of reasoning and distorting a great deal of observation. I am afraid it is going to be difficult to dislodge it from your mind in a few minutes of conversation."

"You can always try."

"Which is exactly what I am prepared to do."

II

He walked across the room and leaned against the bookshelves.

"A great deal has been written about love; but the theorists of love are rare. In fact, since Plato and the guests at the Symposium, there are none that I recognize except Schopenhauer."

"M. de Gourmont has recently written on the subject."

"It amazes me that a man with so shrewd a mind was not able to debunk that last refuge of mysticism, and that his uncompromising skepticism did not recoil from the final metaphysical implications of a theory that makes love the dream of all Nature and the mating instinct the secret spring of life. Also I am amazed that this mind, often so ingenious, was not able to reach the conclusions which I myself am

41

about to advance. His book *The Anatomy of Love* is inspired only by a concern to reduce human love to the level of animal mating; a concern that I shall call zoomorphic, the worthy counterpart of anthropomorphism which rediscovers the tastes and passions of man in everything."

"Why not produce your new theory?"

"I shall, without more ado, in its most monstrous and paradoxical form at first. Later it can be retouched. Here it is: that love is an entirely human invention; that love does not exist in Nature."

"You mean to say, agreeing with de Gourmont, that what we call 'love' is, in fact, nothing but the sexual instinct more or less camouflaged. That may or may not be true, but it is certainly nothing new."

"No, no! I say that the anti-theists, by claiming to replace God by the enormous idol called 'the universal instinct of reproduction' are merely fooling themselves. What de Gourmont is proposing is the *alphysics* of love. I, for my part, claim that this famous 'sexual instinct,' which irresistibly drives one sex towards the other, is of their own invention; this instinct does not exist."

"You need not hope to intimidate me by your peremptory tone. What does your denial of the sexual instinct amount to, at a time when the whole theory of instinct, in its most general form, is being re-examined by Lœb, Bohn, etc.?"

"I did not presume that you were familiar with the detailed work of these men."

"I have not read them all, I admit."

"Or that I was addressing a scholar, rather than someone in whom I thought I detected a certain ignorance in questions of natural history. . . . Oh! don't bother to defend yourself. This ignorance of yours is common enough with literary men. Not being able to make subtle distinctions, nor being able to claim to define in a few words the limits, always very uncertain, of the confines of the word 'instinct,' and knowing that it pleases certain people to see in the words 'sexual instinct' a force both categorically imperative and operating like other instincts with the clear precision of an infallible mechanism,[2] to which de Gourmont says 'obedience is ineluctable,' I say with assurance, 'No, this instinct does not exist!' "

"I see that you are making a play on words. *Really the danger lies,* Bohn wisely remarked in a recent publication, *not in the use of the word 'instinct,' but in the failure to recognize the meaning behind the word, and making it serve as an explanation.* I agree with him. You are actually admitting

43

the existence of the sexual instinct (and my God! you could hardly do otherwise), and are simply denying that it has the automatic precision which some people ascribe to it."

"And it naturally loses more and more precision as one rises in the animal scale."

"So that you would say it was most indeterminate in man."

"We will not discuss man today."

"Whether precise or not, this instinct is transmitted. It has played a rôle and proved itself adequate."

"Yes, adequate . . . exactly."

He stopped and, putting his head in his hands, seemed for a while to be trying to gather his thoughts. Then looking up, he continued:

"By these words 'sexual instinct' one understands a collection of automatisms, or at least of tendencies, which in the lower species are fairly closely knit together, but which, as one ascends the animal scale, are more and more readily and more and more frequently dissociated.

"In order to hold these tendencies together it is often necessary to have a degree of concomitance, connivance, and complicity as I shall explain later—and without these, the unity is lost and the tendencies are allowed to disperse. This instinct is not, so to speak, homogeneous; because the sexual pleasure experienced by both sexes in the act of procreation is not, as you know, necessarily and exclusively linked with that act.

"Whether, in the course of evolution, sexual pleasure precedes or follows the tendency, does not concern me for the moment. I willingly admit that pleasure accompanies each act whereby the vital activity is expressed, so that in the sexual act, which simultaneously involves both great expenditure and the perpetuation of life, pleasure attains its orgasm. . . . And there can be no doubt that this labor of creation, so costly to the individual, would not be achieved without exceptional compensation— but pleasure is not so closely connected with its purpose that it cannot easily be separated and freed.[3] From that moment on, sexual pleasure is pursued for its own sake, without any thought of fertilization. It is not fertilization that animals seek, but simply sexual pleasure. They seek pleasure, and achieve fertilization by accident."

"Of course it needed nothing less than a homosexual to discover a magnificent truth like that."

"Perhaps in fact it did require someone who was disturbed by the prevailing theory. You will notice that Schopenhauer and Plato both realized that they must take account of homosexuality in their theories;

45

they could not do otherwise. Plato indeed assigned so beautiful a rôle to it that I can well understand your feeling alarmed. As for Schopenhauer, whose theory prevails, he only considers it as a kind of exception to his rule, an exception which he explains plausibly but inaccurately, as I shall show you later. In biology, as in physics, I have to admit that exceptions worry me; my mind baulks at them; I have difficulty in understanding a natural law which, only with reservations, can have universal application; a law which permits and even necessitates loopholes."

"So that an outlaw like yourself . . ."

". . . can accept being placed on the Index, and put to shame by the human laws and conventions of his time and country; but cannot accept to live outside the bounds of Nature. That is a contradiction in terms. If there are bounds, then it is because the boundary lines have been imposed too hastily."

"And for your own convenience you would set these boundary lines so as to include and no longer exclude love. Perfect! May I ask, without being impertinent, whether this is entirely your own idea?"

"Others have helped. Reading Lester Ward for instance started the idea, or rather helped to clarify it. Don't worry, I am going to explain; and in the end I hope to show you that my theory, so far from

46

being subversive, actually restores to Love the dignity of which de Gourmont robbed it!"

"This is getting better and better! But I am listening. . . . You referred to . . . ?"

"Lester Ward: an American economist-biologist, supporter of the gynæcocentric theory. I will start by explaining his ideas, and it's here that we reach the heart of the matter."

III

Androcentricity, which Lester Ward treats as the opposite of gynæcocentricity, is scarcely a theory at all, or if it is one, then it is more or less unconsciously so. Androcentricity is the practice, commonly adopted by naturalists, of considering the male as the representative type of each animal species; of giving it first place in descriptions of the species and of treating the female as only secondary.

"Now Lester Ward starts with the point that Nature could if necessary dispense with the male."

"How kind of him."

"In Bergson, whom I know you admire, I have found a passage which answers your interjection: *Sexual generation*, he says in his *Creative Evolution*, *is perhaps superfluous for plants*. The female is certainly indispensable. *The male element*, wrote Lester Ward, *was added at a certain stage . . . for the sole purpose of securing a crossing of ancestral strains. The male is therefore, as it were, a mere afterthought of Nature."*

"Anyway, whether deliberate intention or afterthought, the male is there. Where does your gynæcocentric want him to be relegated?"

"I shall have to take his ideas as a whole. Listen! I think this passage will clarify the meaning of the theory."

He took a sheet of paper and read:

"The normal color of birds is that of the young and the female, and the color of the male is the result of his excessive variability. Females cannot thus vary. They represent the center of gravity of the biological system. They are that 'stubborn power of permanence' of which Goethe speaks. The female not only typifies the race but, metaphor aside, she is the race." [4]

"I don't see anything very curious in that."

"Listen to another passage: *The change, or progress, as it may be called, has been wholly in the male, the female remaining unchanged. This is why it is so often said that the female represents heredity and the male variation.* And Ward quotes the following sentence from W. K. Brooks: *The ovum is the material medium through which the law of heredity manifests itself, while the male element*

49

is the vehicle by which new variations are added.

"Excuse the style. I am not responsible for it."

"Carry on. I pay no attention to that, since I am interested in what he has to say."

"From all this Ward claims to deduce the superiority of the female element. *The idea that the female sex is naturally and really the superior sex seems incredible,* he writes, *and only the most liberal and enlightened people with a serious understanding of biology will be capable of grasping it.* He can say what he likes, but if I do refuse to 'grasp' it, then it is because the conception of superiority seems to me unphilosophical. It is sufficient for me to understand clearly this differentiation of rôles, and I suppose you understand it as I do."

"Go on."

"In support of his thesis, Ward undertakes a kind of history of the male element, as found in the animal species during the various stages of their evolution. With your permission we shall follow him for a moment. He portrays this element as something which is indefinite to begin with and scarcely differentiated in the hermaphrodite condition of cœlenterates; then as something distinct, in the form of a tiny parasite which is carried by the female, fifty or a hundred times larger than itself, as a simple instrument of fertilization, in the same way that certain savage women carry a phallus suspended from their necks.

"Never having heard of these phenomena before, I was astonished."

"Is this natural history serious? Ward is very far-fetched. Can one take his word for it all?"

He rose and went towards the bookcase.

"These animal species and their habits have been known for a long while. Chamisso, the author of *Peter Schlemihl*, was one of the first to deal with them. Here are two volumes of Darwin, dated 1854, which are entirely devoted to the study of cirripedes, an order of animal that for a long time was not distinguished from the molluscs. Most cirripedes are hermaphrodite, but according to Darwin in certain species there are dwarf males, simplified to a point just sufficient for their function; sperm-bearing, without mouths or digestive organs, two, three, or four of them are found on each female. Darwin calls them complementary males. They are equally frequent amongst certain kinds of crustaceous parasites. Look," he said, opening an enormous book on zoology, "this shows you the hideous female of the *Chondracanthus gibbosus*, with her dwarf male attached to her . . .

51

"But from these works I shall only retain what is pertinent to my theory. In this book where I expound it, I show that the male element, after starting by being completely complementary, retains in itself, and tends to retain more and more, all the surplus characteristics which are not employed for the benefit of the race and which can be modified according to the individual—these are the materials of variation."

"I don't follow you. You are going too fast."

"Lester Ward will help: *Throughout the lower orders,* he observes, *an excess of males over females is the normal condition.* Yes, but I in turn have to point out, that in these inferior species, where the males predominate numerically, the male has no purpose other than procreation; he achieves this and expires without accomplishing anything else. Superfluity then consists in the number of individuals, since to fertilize one female a single male is sufficient. Here already we find a useless surplus and, in the form of individuals, material which cannot be employed for the benefit of the species; gratuitous extravagance. In the animal scale, as the number of males in proportion to the number of females is reduced, so this gratuitous surplus becomes concentrated; the individual, so to speak, converts it to his own use. Ward's postulate remains the same: *The essential thing is that no female runs the risk of living unfertilized.* Hence, constant[5] overproduction of the male element—overproduction of males and overproduction of seminal material. But since the female, even with a single egg, is subjugated to the purpose of the race as soon as her fertilization has been accomplished, the male remains unoccupied, well equipped with a strength which soon he will exercise."

"No doubt he will require this strength to protect the race and provide for the wants of the female, since the interests of the race require her to be immobile."

"Let me call Ward to the rescue again. *Nothing is more false,* he writes, *than the oft-repeated statement inspired by the androcentric world view, that the so-called 'superior' males devote that new-gained strength to the work of protecting and feeding the female and the young.* Examples follow. Do you want them?"

"You can lend me the book. Let's go on."

"Not too fast. I have not finished yet."

He put the two volumes of Darwin back on the shelf, sat down again and continued more calmly.

"*The essential thing is that no female runs the risk of living unfertilized.* Yes, but a single male is sufficient to fertilize one female—that is an exaggeration—a single ejaculation, a single spermatozoon is sufficient! Yet the male element is everywhere predominant; either the males are numerically predominant, in so far as the male is exhausted in procreation; or, when the proportion of males is restricted, each male becomes capable of fertilizing a greater number of females. What is this strange mystery? Before studying the cause of it, I would like to show you the consequences."

IV

The first and fatal result among the inferior species is that if the female (as occurs for example amongst the cirripedes) does not allow several males to live with her simultaneously (and even then she has a ridiculously inadequate proportion and only marries one of them), the inevitable result is that a considerable number of males will never experience . . . normal sex, since coitus is denied them; a number considerably greater than those which will be able to satisfy themselves 'normally.' "

"Let us pass on quickly to those species where the proportion of males decreases."

"With them the power of procreation increases, and the problem, instead of confronting the mass, confronts the individual. But the problem remains essentially the same: an overabundance of procreative material; more seed, infinitely more seed, than fields to sow."

"I am afraid you are playing into the hands of the Neo-Malthusians: the males will copulate several times with the same female; several males with one female . . . "

"But usually the female keeps quiet immediately after fecundation."

"I see you are speaking of animals."

"With domestic animals the solution is simple: one stallion is kept for a stable, one cock for a roost, and the remaining males are castrated. Nature however does not castrate. Look at the useless and unpleasant fattening, which the reserve tissues form in castrated animals. Oxen and capons are good for nothing but the table. Castration makes the male into a sort of female. He will take on female characteristics, or, to put it more accurately, he will retain them. But whereas in the female this reserve material is straightway employed for the race, what happens to it in the uncastrated male? Material for variation. Here I believe is the key to what is called 'sexual dimorphism,' which in almost all the so-called 'superior' species makes the male into a creature of show, song, art, sport, or intelligence.

"In Bergson I have come across a remarkable passage," he continued as he rummaged amongst his papers, "which seems to me to throw light on the subject. . . . Ah! here it is. He is dealing with the opposition between the two orders of phenomena which exists in living tissues; *anagenesis* on the one hand and *catagenesis* on the other. *The rôle of anagenetic energies,* he says, *is to raise inferior energies to their proper level for the assimilation of organic substances. They construct the tissues. While on the other hand* . . . but the definition of catagenesis is less striking! You will already have grasped the significance: the rôle of the female is anagenetic; that of the male, catagenetic. Castration, by making a useless anagenetic force prevail in the male, shows how natural for him is a gratuitous expenditure."

"The surplus of elements can, however, only provide material for variation in the uncastrated male, on condition, I think, that it is not expended outside. What I am trying to say is that variation is undoubtedly related directly to the degree of sexual activity."

"I think we must avoid drawing any hasty conclusions. The wisest animal-breeders limit the sexual activity of a stallion to once a day. By a number of unregulated copulations the stallion would be exhausted at a very early age; it would lose its vigor, but it would certainly not lose any of its dimorphic characteristics.[6] The catamorphic force, inhibited in the case of the castrated animal, assumes first place in the complete male."

"I was thinking of the tenors who for the sake of love compromise their top notes . . ."

"The most one can say is that these dimorphic characteristics only reach their fullest development in the so-called 'superior' species, when seminal expenditure is reduced to a minimum. Sexual abstinence, on the contrary, is of no great benefit to the female; no catagenetic force will ever find material for variation in anything she withholds from the race. . . . Listen! Alongside my quotation from Bergson, I find a passage taken from Perrier's speech at the annual session of the Five Academies of 1905. He says nothing very extraordinary, but . . ."

"Read it."

"*If, in the inferior animals, the eggs can obtain possession of these reserves with such avidity that they destroy the creature that has produced them, then one realizes that it is they which check all useless developments in the superior animals; and it is for this reason that the females so often retain permanently the outward trappings of the young, which are only transitional for the male. All this is perfectly co-ordinated.*"

58

"Anagenesis."

"*Everything on the other hand seems to be contrast, contradiction and paradox when it comes to the male sex. Nevertheless this sex also has its characteristics. Its brilliant attire and dazzling methods of courtship are in short nothing but a vain display of dead parts, the sign of a senseless outlay, of an inordinate waste of the organism, the mark of a temperament which can exteriorize but which knows no economy.*"

"Catagenesis."

"*The sumptuous coloring of butterflies is to be found in tiny scales, exquisite no doubt, but quite lifeless. . . . the coloring of birds develops in feathers which are completely dead,* etc. I cannot read you the whole speech."

"And did not sculpture and painting develop in the same way, on precisely those parts of Greek temples and of cathedrals which had ceased to serve any practical purpose?"

"Yes, this is how one explains the formation, for instance, of triglyphs and metopes. One might say that only things which have ceased to have practical use can serve any æsthetic purpose. But let's not insist on this. It will only distract us.

"*The female sex,* Perrier concluded, *is in some*

59

ways the sex of physiological foresight; the male sex
that. of. extravagant. but. unproductive. expenditure . . ."

"This surely is where natural selection comes
in? Did not Darwin say that all things, like the song
of nightingales, beautiful coloring, amazing forms,
were there simply to attract the female?"

"Here I go back to Ward. You must excuse so
many quotations, but the theory I am attempting to
formulate is hazardous, and I must ensure certain
points of support.

"*The female is the guardian of hereditary quali-
ties. Variation can be excessive . . . She requires
regulation. The woman is the balancing force of
Nature . . .*

"And elsewhere: *While the voice of Nature,
speaking to the male in the form of an intense appe-
titive interest says to him: fecundate! it gives to the
female a different command, and says: discriminate!*

"To tell you the truth, I distrust this 'voice of
Nature.' To remove God from creation and replace
Him by 'voices' . . . that's a fine improvement.
Endowing Nature with eloquence appears to be
a case of the old maxim that 'Nature abhors a
vacuum'! This sort of scientific mysticism seems
as inauspicious for science as it is for religion. But
it does not matter! Taking the word 'voice' in its

most metaphorical sense, I still deny that it says to the male: fecundate! and to the female: discriminate! It simply says to both sexes: enjoy! It is the voice of the glands which demands satisfaction; the organs which crave employment—organs which have been formed in accordance with the requirements of their precise function, but which are guided by the sole need of pleasure. Nothing more.

"Logically speaking, it is less difficult to accept the supposed choice of the female; but in most cases it is the best-qualified male that wins her and that she is forced to choose—as the result of elimination."

He was silent for a moment as though at a loss. Then he re-lit the cigarette which he had allowed to go out and continued:

"We have briefly examined the consequences of the overproduction of the male element (and I propose to return to it in the second part of my book, which I shall explain to you tomorrow, if you like); in the meantime, we will try and ascertain the cause of it."

V

I use the word 'prodigality' for all expenditure which is out of proportion to the result achieved. Several pages of my book will deal, in a general way, with prodigality in Nature: prodigality in forms; prodigality in numbers. Today we will deal only with the latter. The surplus number of eggs to begin with; then the superabundance of seminal material.

"The large white Doris (a sort of sea-slug) lays approximately 600,000 eggs, according to Darwin's 'most moderate computation.' *Yet this Doris was not very common,* he wrote, *although I was often searching under the stones, I saw only seven individuals.*' This prodigality in the number of eggs does not in any way imply a wide diffusion of the species, in favor of which it is exercised. On the contrary it often seems to imply a *difficulty in succeeding* proportionate to the prodigality expended. Darwin then added that *No fallacy is more common with naturalists than that the numbers of an individual species depend on its power of propagation.*[8] It is fair to suppose that with some hundred fewer eggs, the Doris species would become extinct.

"Elsewhere Darwin speaks of the way in which conifers have clouds of pollen carried to them by the wind, and of how they are smothered with *these thick clouds of pollen, simply in order that a few grains can fall by chance on the ovules.* If one were to attribute to the pollen grain some instinct, whereby it was guided to the ovule, then there would be no explanation, no excuse for such profusion. But perhaps with a smaller proportion of the male element, the mysterious act of fertilization would remain too much a matter of chance.[9]

"Is not the explanation, the *raison d'être* of this almost constant superabundance of the male element[10] to be found in a certain indecision of the sexual instinct (if I dare couple the words 'indecision' and 'instinct')? Will it not soon have to be admitted that the imperative quality of this instinct is really rather ambiguous? And is not Nature comparable to a marksman who, knowing his lack of skill and fearing to miss the target, compensates for the inaccuracy of his aim by the number of shots he fires?"

"I did not think you were a finalist."

"In point of fact the 'wherefore' concerns me less than the 'how.' But it is often fairly hard to disentangle the two questions. Nature constitutes a network without beginning or end, and one is uncertain in which direction one should tackle this unbroken chain. Nothing is more problematical than the question as to whether the *raison d'être* of each link is to be found in the link which precedes or the link which succeeds it (if indeed it has a *raison d'être* at all), and whether the entire book of Nature, to be properly understood, should not be read from back to front—in other words, whether the last page is not the explanation of the opening, the last link the secret motive of the first. . . . The finalist is the man who reads the book from back to front."

"For heaven's sake, no metaphysics!"

"Do you want the preceding link explanation? Would you be satisfied if some biologist came along and told us that the overproduction of males is caused by insufficiency of nourishment—after previously proving, for example, that an overabundance of food tends to produce a greater proportion of females (I do not know if this is a duly established fact[11]), but that such an overabundance of food is never realized in the natural state of affairs,

64

or at any rate never for long. Well, suppose that this overabundance did exist and lead in accordance with this theory to an overproduction of females: then, either a certain number of these females would run the risk of living unfertilized (which is contrary to Ward's first postulate), or they would all be fertilized, in which case the overproduction of individuals in the following generation would result in a shortage of food, which, in its turn, would result in a greater proportion of males, so that in two generations the equilibrium would be restored. For in principle one can assume, providing no decimating factor interrupts, that there is never too much food and there is always the maximum number of mouths to be fed from Nature's store. How does this explanation please you?"

"Well, anyway . . . let's try the 'succeeding link' explanation."

"All right. We will tackle the chain from the other end. If I maintain that the sexual instinct is inadequate, yes: insufficiently precise to assure the perpetuation of the species, then the surplus of males can be considered as a necessary precaution . . ."

"Or rather let us say that any species in which the number of males remains insufficient becomes extinct."

"If you like. After moving from opposite directions, the finalist and the evolutionist arrive at this same point. The excess of males is necessary for the perpetuation of the race *because* the sexual instinct is inadequate."

"That is the point which still has to be established."

"In a moment we are going to prove its inadequacy in Nature; but first of all I would like to examine with you the possible causes of this flagrant insufficiency. Let us proceed step by step."

"I am with you. You said: with a smaller proportion of the male element the act of fecundation might have remained too much a matter of chance."

"It is certainly a hazardous business. You have two elements, male and female, which have to be joined together, with no inducement other than sexual pleasure. But the joining of the two sexes is not an indispensable condition for obtaining this pleasure. No doubt the male is necessary for the fertilization of the female; but the female is not indispensable for the satisfaction of the male. This famous 'sexual instinct' may well dictate to the animal the automatism whereby sexual pleasure can be obtained, but its directive is so indecisive that, in order at the same time to ensure procreation, Nature must on occasions have recourse to ruses as

66

subtle as in the case of the fortuitous fertilization of orchids."

"Again you are speaking as a finalist."

"You must excuse me. Creation is there. Whether it could possibly not be there, I do not know. But it *is*. The only thing to do is to explain it as economically as possible. We are faced with races of creatures that are perpetuated by reproduction, and that can only reproduce by fecundation. It is, I say, a difficult business, a reckless gamble and the chances of failure are so tremendous that this surplus of males was undoubtedly necessary to offset the number of fiascos."

"You see, Nature's *intention* reappearing."

"My metaphor has misled you. Perhaps there is a God, but there is certainly no *intention* in Nature. I mean that if there is any such intention, then it can be none other than that of God. There is no intention in sexual pleasure, which is the sole motive for that act whereby procreation is possible; and whether it preceded or followed the inclination, I still say that it has freed itself, become an end in itself and is now entirely self-sufficient.[12]

"Was it not Chamfort who reduced love to the 'contact of two epidermis'?"

"And to the exchange of two fantasies."

67

"Let's leave fantasy for human beings; for animals there is nothing but the sensual pleasure of contact."

"Are you going so far as to say that the sexual instinct reduces itself to that?"

"No! But that without the assistance of special expedients, which I shall describe to you in a moment, it is not certain—as you have intermittently tried to maintain—it is not always assured that the male will choose the female and achieve fecundation. That, I tell you, is an arduous business and Nature will not achieve it without the intervention of favorable factors."

VI

This theory was too new for my taste, and for a while I was reduced to silence; but I quickly recovered:

"Good heavens! Corydon, you are joking! No sexual instinct! I am no great natural history scholar, it is true, and I realize that I am not particularly observant, but down in the country, where I spend the autumn hunting, I have seen the dogs come from the neighboring village, more than a kilometer away and spend the entire night around my fence, barking at my bitch . . ."

"That must disturb your sleep."

"Fortunately it only lasts a short while."

"Is that so. Why?"

"My bitch, thank God, does not remain in heat for long."

I immediately regretted my remark for, on

catching it, Corydon assumed a bantering tone which made me uneasy. But I had already gone too far not to answer, when he continued:

"And this lasts . . . ?"

"About a week."

"And occurs?"

"Twice, perhaps three times, a year . . ."

"And at other times?"

"Corydon, I am getting impatient. What are you trying to make me say?"

"That at other times the dogs leave the bitch alone—you know that as well as I do. Except at set periods it is impossible to cover a bitch with a dog (and, incidentally it is not always so easy even at the right times)—first of all because the bitch refuses and secondly because the male shows absolutely no desire." [13]

"Ah, exactly! Is it not precisely the sexual instinct which warns them that at these times there could be no fertilization?"

"What well-educated animals! And no doubt it is out of virtue that your enlightened dog abstains at ordinary times?"

"There are numbers of animals that only make love in times of rut."

"What you mean is that females only make love. . . . Because if, poetically speaking, there is a season of love, then it is not, properly speaking, a season for the males (in particular dogs which we are considering at the moment and in general all domestic animals have little regard for seasons). For the male all seasons are good; for the female only special periods. And it is only then that the male desires her.[14] Would not this attraction be due to the odor which the female gives off at those periods? [15] Would it not be this smell, rather than the bitch herself, which causes the dogs of the neighboring village to come flocking to the subtle odor and which keeps them awake although they cannot reach her . . . ?"

"It is a combination of the two. As the smell could not exist without the bitch . . ."

"But if, after establishing that the bitch without this smell does not excite the dog, we go on to establish that this smell will excite the dog independently of the bitch, will we not then have made that kind of *experimentum crucis* of which Bacon would approve?"

"What ridiculous experiment are you now suggesting?"

"The one that Rabelais so obscenely, or rather so accurately, relates in the second book of Pantagruel (chapter XXII). There we read how Pantagruel, to avenge himself for a certain lady's unkind-

71

ness, secured a bitch in heat, cut her up, tore out the ovaries and, having thoroughly crushed them, made a kind of ointment to spread on the cruel woman's dress. Here I will let Rabelais describe it in his own words."

Rising, Corydon proceeded to fetch the book from his shelves and read the following passage:

" .   .   .   .
.   .   .   .
.   .   .   .   .   ."

"Should that be treated as anything more than a fantasy?"

"Which in itself would not be enough to convince us," he continued. "But Nature is constantly providing us with equally conclusive examples.[16] This smell is so strong and disturbing to animal senses that it exceeds the rôle assigned to it by sexuality (if I dare use such an expression) and like a simple aphrodisiac intoxicates not only the male but also other females that come close to a female in rut and even makes them attempt clumsy approaches.[17] Farmers separate a cow in season from the rest of the herd when it is being molested by other cows . . .[18] And this finally is the point I wish to make: that if the sexual appetite of the male is aroused by the periodic odor of the female, then that is not the only time at which it is aroused." [19]

"It has been maintained, and with reason I presume, that the male can actually excite other males by carrying on him the smell of a recent coitus and therefore the evocative associations of a female."

"It would certainly be strange if this smell, which disappears so quickly from the female, in fact according to Samson 'immediately after fecundation,' [20] should persist when transferred to another . . . but be that as it may! I can assure you that I have seen dogs assiduously pursue other dogs which have never had coitus; and they resume the pursuit at each fresh encounter without any regard for season."

"If the facts you give are accurate—and I agree to accept them as such . . ."

"You can hardly do otherwise."

"How do you explain the fact that no account has been taken of them in the Record of Scientific Facts?"

"First of all because no such 'Record' exists. Also because to date there has been very little observation of the things I am telling you. And finally because it is as difficult and rare to observe well as to think or write well. In order to become a great scholar it is sufficient to be a good observer. The great man of science is just as rare as other men of genius. There are numerous half-scholars who will accept a traditional theory to guide or misguide them, and which they will use as the basis of all their 'observations.' For a long time everything confirmed Nature's abhorrence of a vacuum; yes, all the *observations*. For a long time everything confirmed the existence of two different electricities, with a sort of almost sexual instinct attracting them. At present, everything once again confirms this theory of the 'sexual instinct.' . . . So that the stupefaction of certain breeders, on discovering the homosexual habits of the animals with which they deal, is really laughable. Each of these modest 'observers,' confining his attention to his own particular species, believes these habits must be taken as monstrous exceptions. We read in Havelock Ellis that 'pigeons appear to be particularly prone to sexual perversion, if we are to believe M. J. Bailly the competent breeder and *excellent observer*';[21] and that Muccioli 'the learned Italian, *who is an authority on pigeons*, states that the practices of inversion are found amongst Belgian carrier pigeons, *even in the presence of many females*.' "

"What? The Two Pigeons of La Fontaine . . . ?"

"Don't worry; they were French pigeons. Someone else observes the same habits amongst ducks, being a breeder of ducks. Lacassagne, dealing with chickens, observes them amongst chickens. Was it not amongst young partridges that Bouvard or Pécuchet claimed to come across these habits? . . . Yes, there is nothing funnier than these timid and tentative observations, unless it is the conclusions which some people draw from them, or the explanations they give for them. Dr. X., having proved the great frequency of intercourse between male cockchafers, then produces arguments to excuse their wickedness."

"Yes, it is what I was telling you a moment ago: only the male which has just copulated and which is still impregnated with the odor of the female, can offer any pretext for assault . . ."

"Is Dr. X. quite certain of what he says? Was it really after copulation that males in their turn were covered? Did he scrupulously *observe* it, or did he conveniently *assume* it? . . . I suggest this experiment: I would like to know whether a dog, deprived of all sense of smell, would not in consequence be condemned to . . ."

"To homosexuality pure and simple."

"Or at least to celibacy, to the complete absence of heterosexual desires. . . . But just because the dog does not desire the bitch except when she is in good odor, it does not necessarily follow from this, that his desires are dormant the rest of the time.

75

Hence the great frequency of homosexual activity."

"Let me in turn ask: have you scrupulously *observed* it, or are you conveniently *assuming* it?"

"You could easily observe it for yourself; but I know that usually people who pass and see from a distance two dogs copulating assume the sex of each from the position it occupies.[22] Dare I tell you this story? On one of the Paris boulevards two dogs were stuck in the pitiful fashion that sometimes occurs. They were both satisfied and were struggling to free themselves. Their efforts scandalized some people and provided great amusement for others. I approached. Three male dogs were prowling around the group, undoubtedly attracted by the smell. One of them, bolder or more excited than the others, could hold back no longer and tried to assault the couple. I watched him for some time perform the most incredible antics, in his attempt to mount one of the captives. Most of us were there, I say, to watch this scene out of more or less good motives; but I guarantee I was the only one to notice that it was the male and only the male that the dog wanted to mount. He deliberately ignored the female. He did all he could to achieve his purpose and as the other dog, being attached, could scarcely resist, he had almost succeeded . . . when a policeman appeared on the scene and dispersed both dogs and spectators."

"May I suggest that the theory which you put forward and which was no doubt prompted by your temperament—that this theory preceded the strange observations you have recounted, and that you have yourself given way to the temptation you so vehemently criticize in your scientific colleagues: of observing in order to prove."

"One has to admit right away, that it is very difficult to suppose that an *observation* can be the result of chance, and that it reaches the brain as the accidental answer to a question which the brain would not have formulated. The important thing is not to force the answer. Have I succeeded? I hope so; but I cannot be absolutely certain, being as fallible as others. All I ask is that the answers, which Nature whispers or shouts to me, be verified. Finally what I want to emphasize is this, that having investigated Nature from a different standpoint, I received a different set of answers."

"Could not the investigation be conducted from a natural standpoint?"

"In this particular connection, it seems to me to be difficult. For example, Sainte-Claire Deville says he has *observed* that goats, rams or dogs shut away from females grow agitated and excited amongst themselves, 'with a sexual excitement which no longer depends on the laws of rut and which drives them to intercourse.' I beg you to notice the exquisite euphemism: 'which no longer depends on the laws of rut.' Sainte-Claire Deville adds: 'It is sufficient to introduce a female to restore order.' Is he really sure of that? Has he really observed it? He is *convinced* of it, which is not at all the same thing. This example is taken from a report to the Academy of Moral Sciences on 'the boarding school and its influence on the education of the young.' Does he speak from knowledge, or only as a pedagogue? And is it necessary that this female of salvation, whom he introduces into the kennel or stable where the laws of rut have been broken, should always be in heat? If she is not, then we know that the dogs will not approach her; and if instead of one female twenty were introduced, they would still continue their pursuit of one another without caring about the females."

"Perhaps Sainte-Claire Deville's observations were wrong from the start."

"Nonsense. Sainte-Claire Deville's initial observations of the homosexual activities of these animals were perfectly sound. It was from then on that his flagrant inventions began. If he had agreed to push his investigations further, he could have discovered that the introduction of one or more individuals of the opposite sex was definitely not sufficient to restore order, except for about one week of the year when these females were able to arouse excitement; and that the rest of the time these homosexual activities continued 'even in the presence of many females,' as Muccioli says."

"No doubt you consider this lascivious sport the most innocent of pastimes."

"Although this play may have the greatest signif-icance, one can say that these animals do not find, or only on very rare occasions, complete satisfaction in homosexuality. How inexorable then this desire must be, to drive them to it all the same."

"Of course you know," I said unwisely, "that bitches do not always surrender willingly, even when they are in heat. The bitch I was telling you about a moment ago was a thoroughbred. I wanted her to have a litter. With great trouble I secured a male of the same breed; but when the time came to cover her, what a business! First of all the bitch tried to escape. The dog was exhausting himself in clumsy efforts. Then when she appeared docile, the dog completely refused. . . . It was only at the end of five days that we succeeded in having her covered."

"Excuse me," he said smiling, "but are you producing this as evidence against my theory?"

I could not withdraw. "I contribute my share of impartial observations," I said, "to the subject under discussion."

"Thank you . . . yes, all breeders know of these difficulties. On farms numerous inseminations have to be assisted and the sexual instinct appears in the guise of a farmhand."

"Well then, how is it done in Nature?"

VII

For the past hour I have been explaining to you that this is why the male element is so abundant. Your famous 'sexual instinct' makes up for its imprecision by multiplying its incidence. On farms where one keeps an exactly adequate number of stallions, the gamble would be too great if men did not sometimes direct operations. In Samson's course on animal technology there are no less than nine pages devoted solely to the serving of horses. For the stallion, he informs his students at Grignon, 'easily loses its way'; and 'when it has reared, the groom has to seize the penis with his hand to guide it,' etc.

"But, as you have said, the difficulty does not arise only from the clumsiness of the male; the female, for her part, becomes restive and tries to escape, so that it is often necessary to hold her. Two explanations have been given for this remarkable dread. The first consists of ascribing to the animal the human sentiments of Galatea, of inflaming the desires of the male by a pretense of flight. The second consists of ascribing to Galatea the sensations of the animal, which simultaneously desires and dreads . . ."

"Is it not probable that the two explanations coincide?"

"I assure you that certain people do not seem to have noticed it; and once again de Gourmont proposes the second as opposed to the first."

"You no doubt have a third?"

"Yes. It is that the sexual instinct is as indecisive in the female, as it is in the male. . . . The female will only feel *complete* when fecundated; but if, as a result of a secret need of the organs, she craves for fecundation, then it is vaguely sexual pleasure and not precisely the male that she desires; just as the male, on his side, does not desire precisely the female, and still less 'procreation,' but simply sexual pleasure. Both of them quite plainly seek pleasure.

"And that is the reason why we so often see the female fleeing the male, while at the same time offering herself for pleasure, until finally she returns to the male, who alone can provide her with it. I agree that it is only with each other that they can experience complete satisfaction (at least the female only

82

with the male) and that their organs will only find perfect employment in coitus. But it seems that they do not know it—or only in such a confused manner that ordinarily it scarcely amounts to an instinct.

"But, for fecundation to operate, it is necessary to make these two drifting desires converge at least once. Hence the persuasive aroma spread by the female at suitable times, whereby she indicates unmistakably her presence to the male; an aroma, or some even subtler emanation, to which the antennæ of insects are sensitive; which, in the case of certain fish, for example, is not even spread by the female, but by the eggs which are fertilized direct by the male, so that the female seems to be excluded from the game of love.

"It is through a single door, narrowly ajar for an instant, that the future must insinuate itself. For such an incredible victory over disorder and death, Nature has been granted 'prodigality.' In this there is assuredly no 'thoughtless expenditure,' for to incur such waste is not to pay too dearly for the triumph. . . ."

" 'Waste' you said?"

"Yes, waste, from a utilitarian point of view. But it is on this waste that art, thought and play will be able to flourish. And as we saw the two forces, anagenetic and catagenetic, set in opposition to each other, so now in the same way we shall see two possible forms of devotion: that of the female for the race; that of the male for his art, his sport, his song. Can you think of any drama more beautiful than this, in which two forms of devotion confront each other in sublime conflict?"

"Are we not encroaching on tomorrow's conversation? Anyway, before leaving the subject of natural history I would like to ask you some more questions. Do you claim that homosexual tastes are found in all animal species?"

"In many, but perhaps not in all. I cannot say too much, for lack of sufficient information. . . . However, I very much doubt whether they are to be found in those species where coitus is most difficult, or at any rate where it is most complicated and necessitates great effort; with dragonflies, for example, or certain types of spider which practice a sort of artificial insemination; or with others where the male, either immediately after coitus, or even during coitus, is devoured by the female. . . . Here, I tell you, I make no assertions. I have to content myself with supposition."

"A strange supposition."

"Perhaps, in order to establish it as a fact, it would be sufficient to prove that in species where

84

coitus is acrobatic or dangerous, the male element is proportionately smaller. I was rather startled by some words of Fabre: *In the second half of August I began to encounter the adult insect. . . . Day by day the pregnant females became more frequent. Their frail companions are on the other hand rather rare and I sometimes have considerable difficulty in completing my pairs.* Here he is speaking of the praying mantis, in which the male is always devoured.

"This scarcity of male element ceases to appear paradoxical, if it is compensated for by the precision of the instinct. Since the male must be sacrificed by the female, it is essential that the desire which drives him to coitus should be compelling and precise; and *once that desire has acquired precision, the excess of males becomes unnecessary.* On the other hand, it is essential that the number of males[24] increases as soon as the instinct slackens; and the instinct slackens as soon as the danger is removed from sexual pleasure; or at least when sexual pleasure becomes easy.

"So the disturbing axiom: that the number of males diminishes as the difficulty of coitus increases, is after all nothing but the natural corollary of what I first advanced: that the surplus of males (or the overabundance of the male element) is compensation for the imprecision of the instinct; or if you prefer: that

85

the imprecision of the instinct finds its justification in the overabundance of the male element; or again . . ."

"I have understood."

"I insist on making my points clear:

"1. As coitus is more difficult, so the instinct is proportionately more precise.

"2. As the instinct is more precise, so the number of males is proportionately less.

"3. Therefore the number of males diminishes as the difficulty of coitus increases (for those males which are sacrificed); so that if there were some other way of achieving sexual pleasure, then there is no doubt they would abandon immediately the dangers of coitus—and the species would become extinct. But undoubtedly Nature has left them no other means of satisfaction.[25]

"Again, I am only making suppositions."

"Let's consider this. As I come to understand you better, it grows increasingly clear that your conclusion appreciably exceeds your premises. I admit I am indebted to you for making me reconsider these matters, which are usually governed by a sort of authoritarian principle, imposing a ready-made set of beliefs that one carefully refrains from questioning. Here then is the point I reach with you:

"Yes, the sexual instinct does exist, in spite of what you say. It operates, although you will not have it so, with precision and extraordinary insistence; but it is only compelling at the correct time, at the moment when the two elements come into play. In order to ensure that the female's momentary demands meet with instant response, she is confronted with the permanent desire of the male. The male, you have said, is wholly gratuitous; the female is full of foresight. The only heterosexual contact (of animals) is for the purpose of fecundation."

"And the male is not always content with that."

"For some time we have been losing sight of your book. Have you any conclusions to draw from this first part?"

"Just this, which I put to the finalists: if, in spite of the almost constant overabundance of the male element, Nature still requires so many expedients and artificial aids to ensure the perpetuation of the race, will it surprise us to learn that just as many restraints, and of just as many kinds, may be required to check the propensity of the human race for those habits which you have termed 'abnormal'; and that just as many arguments, examples, inducements and encouragements may be needed to maintain the desired ratio of human heterosexuality?"

87

"But will you grant me that there is some good in this restraint on the one side, and this encouragement on the other?"

"I will grant it until tomorrow, when we shall examine the question, no longer from a zoological, but from a human point of view, and we shall consider whether perhaps repression and excitation have not gone too far. But, in return, will you for your part admit that homosexual habits no longer seem so unnatural as you claimed this morning? That is all I ask of you today."

THIRD DIALOGUE

I have thought a lot since yesterday," I said to Corydon on entering. "But tell me, do you really believe the theory you put forward?"

"At least I am fully convinced of the facts which prompted it. As for claiming that the explanation I offer for them is the only possible one, or is even the best, far be it from me to be so presumptuous. But I shall add that, in my opinion, this is of no great importance. What I mean is, that the importance of a newly advanced system, of a new explanation for certain phenomena, is not to be assessed solely on its accuracy but also, and above all, on the impetus it provides to the spirit for fresh discoveries and new appraisals (should the latter invalidate the said theory), on the channels it opens, on the barriers it removes, on the weapons it furnishes. The essential thing is that it proposes the new and at the same time opposes the old. Today it may seem to us that the whole of Darwin's theory is being shaken to its very foundations. Shall we for that reason deny that Darwinism, in its day, constituted a great advance in science? Shall we say that De Vries is right as opposed to Darwin? No; no more than that Darwin or even Lamarck were right as opposed to X."

"According to you, one could not even venture to say that Galileo . . ."

"Allow me to make a distinction between statements of fact and the explanation that one gives those facts. The explanation remains flexible; but so far from always following the new observations, it often precedes them. Sometimes, in fact often, we find theory ahead of observation and it is only later that observations confirm the daring propositions of the mind. Take, for example, my own theories. If you will only acknowledge that they show a certain initiative, then I shall be satisfied. Once again facts are there which you cannot deny. As for the explanation that I give for them, I am ready to renounce it as soon as you produce a better."

I

Yesterday we were able to consider," he continued, "the preponderant rôle played by the sense of smell, the sense which guides the instincts in animal intercourse. Thanks to this, the indefinite desire of the male is deliberately directed towards the female —and solely towards the female in rut. One can say, without too much exaggeration, that the 'sexuality' of the genetic instinct (to use modern jargon) lies in the olfactory sense of the male. Properly speaking, there is no selection of the female by the male; as soon as she becomes in heat, he is drawn towards her, led by the nose. Lester Ward, in a passage I have not read to you, emphasizes the fact that 'all females are the same, for the male animal'; and actually, as we have seen, they all *are* the same, only the male being capable of variation and individualization. The female, to attract him, has no resources other than her smell; she has no need of other attractions; she does not have to be beautiful; it is sufficient that she be in good odor. Choice—if choice is not simply the victory of the fittest—choice remains the privilege of the female. She may choose according to her taste and there we touch on æsthetics. It is the female, Lester Ward insists, who exercises the power of selection and who in consequence creates what he calls the 'efflorescence of the male.' For the moment I shall not attempt to determine whether this superior beauty of the individual male in the majority of insects, birds, fishes and mammals and which may be the result of the female's good taste, is to be found also in the human race."

"I have been waiting a long time for you to reach this."

"Provisionally, since you are impatient, let me draw attention to the fact that the male nightingale's coloring is not much brighter than the female's; but the latter does not sing. The efflorescence of the male is not necessarily decorative. It is exuberant, and perhaps it is in song, in certain sports or in intelligence that it finally appears.

"But let me keep to the order of my book, in which I broach this important question later on."

"Follow whatever order you like. I agree to your deferring all embarrassing questions, providing you

94

come to them in the end. For I am determined from now on not to let you drop the subject until you have exhausted your science and your logic and fired all your arguments. But tell me how you begin the second part of your book?"

"All right. I begin by stating that the sense of smell, which is of such capital importance in the intercourse of animals, plays no further rôle in the sexual relations of human beings. If it does intervene, then it is for supererogatory reasons."

"Is that really such a very interesting observation?"

"To me this difference seems so remarkable, that I can hardly believe that de Gourmont, by making no mention of it in his book and taking no account of it in his assimilation of man with animals, could really have failed to notice it, or would have simply omitted it—or very conveniently conjured it out of sight."

"I have never yet seen him embarrassed by an objection. Perhaps he did not attach quite the same importance to it that you do."

"Its importance will become apparent to you, I hope, when you appreciate its consequences, which I will try to explain to you.

"Let us put it this way. The woman no longer has the periodic odor of the menses with which to attract the man. Other attractions, no doubt, take its place. These attractions, whether natural or artificial, are not dependent on seasons and are not governed by ovulation. The desirable woman is desirable at all times. Let us go further. Whereas the male animal only desires the female and she only permits his approaches during the periods of heat, man, on the other hand, usually abstains during the menstrual periods. Not only are these periods devoid of attraction, but they entail a sort of prohibition. For the moment I am not concerned with whether this is physical or moral, whether one must see it as a temporary disgust of the flesh, a survival of ancient religious precepts or a disapproval of the spirit—the fact remains that from here on man is separated, and clearly separated, from the animals.

"Henceforth the sexual appetite, while still remaining all-powerful, is no longer attached so closely to the olfactory nerves which hitherto held it on a leash. Now it has wider scope. Love (and I am loath to use this word already, but I have to sooner or later), love at once turns into a game—a sport without closed season."

"Which does not mean to say, I hope, that everyone is absolutely free to play it as he pleases."

"No, for the desire will remain no less compelling. At least it will be more diverse. For the imperative to be as categorical, it will become more particular; yes, particular for each individual. And furthermore the individual will no longer crave vaguely for the female, but for one woman in particular.

"Spinoza said that *The affections of animals differ from the affections of men, as much as their nature differs from man's*; and further on when he is speaking more especially of humanity, that *The pleasures of one man are as distinct from the pleasures of another as the nature of the one differs from the nature of the other—adeo gaudium unius a gaudio alterius tantum natura discrepat, quantum essentia unius ab essentia alterius differt.*"

"Montaigne, Pascal and now Spinoza. You certainly know how to pick your sponsors. This '*gaudium unius*,' interpreted by you, tells me nothing of value. As Pascal said, 'I am very much afraid.' . . . But go on."

He smiled and then began again.

II

On the one hand constant attraction; on the other hand selection, no longer exercised by the female in favor of the male, but by the man in favor of the woman. . . . Have we not here the key to, or rather the justification of, the otherwise inexplicable pre-eminence of feminine elegance?"

"What do you mean by that?"

"That from top to bottom of the animal scale, we have had to acknowledge the astonishing supremacy of male beauty (for which I have tried to offer the explanation); that it is therefore rather disconcerting to find in human beings a sudden reversal of this hierarchy; and the reasons one has been able to find for this sudden reversal are either mystical or impertinent—to such a point that certain skeptics have asked whether woman's beauty did not reside principally in man's desire, and whether . . ."

I did not allow him to finish. I was so unprepared to hear him produce arguments based on common sense that at first I did not catch his meaning. But as soon as I did, I was determined not to give him time to retract and exclaimed:

"You have helped us out of a difficulty, and I must thank you. I now realize that this 'constant attraction' of women begins precisely where the other leaves off; and it is obviously of no small importance that man's desire is no longer dependent on his sense of smell, but on his more artistic and less subjective sense of sight; and this no doubt is what permits the development of culture and art . . ."

I then let myself go with the confidence which this first sign of good sense had inspired in me.

"It is rather ironical to owe to a homosexual the first sensible argument in favor of what you call the 'pre-eminent elegance of the fair sex.' For I have to admit that up till now I have been unable to find any other, except in my own sentiments. I shall now be able to reread, without embarrassment, certain passages from Perrier's speech to the Academy, which you lent me yesterday . . ."

"What passages are you alluding to?"

Pulling the pamphlet from my pocket, I read:

"*To watch the caressing colors of fine dresses, playing in the summer sunlight or under the chan-*

99

deliers of a great ballroom . . . one would think that adornment had been the exclusive invention of the daughters of Eve; the silver, the gold, the diamonds, the flowers, the feathers, the butterfly wings . . . ! Men have not yet dared to trespass on the 'creation' of these jewels, in which women's imaginations and their love of coquetry seem to express themselves. Their hats, so exquisite witty or triumphal . . ."

"You have to excuse him. He probably saw all this at some fashionable gathering."

"There is an increasingly sharp distinction, at any rate in our civilized countries, between women's taste for decorative apparel and men's detached attitude towards all forms of studied elegance . . ."

"That is what I told you: that the efflorescence of the male is not necessarily decorative."

"Wait till I have finished reading . . . *Even the somber costume of the middle class seems to be too cumbersome. It is made lighter and shorter, until it is reduced to a simple jacket; so that at ceremonies where women are present, we appear like humble insects gliding amongst flowers."*

"Flattering!"

"This evolution is absolutely characteristic. It separates the human race from the higher animals, as much as any of its physical or psychological char-

acteristics. *It is, in fact, the exact opposite of what oc-*
curs in most of the animal world, where the male is
in all respects the favored sex, even in the lowest
forms of life."

"Is that the passage which embarrassed you?
May I ask why? For it seems to me, on the contrary,
that it ought to have pleased you . . ."

"Don't assume such innocence! As though it had
escaped your notice that Perrier, while pretending to
extol the fair sex, is really only extolling the veneer." [1]

"Yes; what I called just now the 'artificial attractions.' "

"The words strike me as being dishonest; but I
see what you mean. And now that I come to think of
it, it is not very smart for a clever man to over-insist
on this point; because to say to a woman: 'What a
charming hat you have' is not, after all, as flattering
as to say: 'How beautiful you are.' "

"It is even better to say: 'How becoming your
hat is.' But is this all that upsets you? I seem to remember that Perrier, towards the end of his speech,
drops the question of adornments and starts to praise
the person who wears them. Give me the speech.
Listen: *Ladies, you have triumphed with the clarity*
of your complexions, the crystal purity of your
voices, the gentle elegance of your gestures and those

graceful lines which have inspired the brush of Bouguereau. What could you want prettier than that? Why did you not read those lines?"

"Because I knew you did not like Bouguereau."

"You are really too considerate!"

"Stop mocking and tell me what you think of all this."

"I admit that, in effect, so much artifice so constantly summoned to the assistance of Nature, upsets me. I recollect a passage from Montaigne in which he says: *It is not so much modesty as artistry and prudence which causes our women to be so circumspect in forbidding us to enter their closets before they are painted and prepared for their appearance in public.* I have come to doubt whether, in Pierre Louys' fantasy, *Tryphème,* the custom of frankly exhibiting the advantages of the fair sex, and the habit of displaying themselves stark naked about the town and over the countryside, would not produce a contrary effect to what he seems to predict, and whether man's desire for the opposite sex would not be considerably cooled. *It remains to be seen,* said Mademoiselle Quinault, *whether all the objects which excite in us so many beautiful and wicked thoughts because they are hidden from view would not leave us cold, if we had to contemplate them perpetually; for there are examples of such things.* After all, there are tribes, and they are actually the handsomest, where the dream of Tryphème is realized (or at least it was fifty years ago, before the work of the missionaries), as for example Tahiti at the time when Darwin landed there in 1835. In a few moving pages he describes the splendor of the natives and then adds: *I was much disappointed in the personal appearance of the women; they are far inferior in every respect to the men* . . . Then after declaring that they required adornments² to compensate for this lack of beauty, he continued: *The women appear to be in greater want of some becoming costume even than the men.*"

"I was not aware that Darwin was a homosexual."

"Whoever said he was?"

"Wouldn't one gather so from this passage?"

"What? Are you forcing me to take de Gourmont seriously when he writes: *It is the woman who represents beauty. Any divergent opinion will be held eternally either as a paradox or as the product of the most annoying of sexual aberrations.*"

" 'Eternally' seems too strong for you?"

"Keep calm. As far as I know, Darwin was no more a homosexual than many other explorers who, traveling among naked tribes, marveled at the beauty of the young men—no more a homosexual than Stevenson, for example, who, speaking of the Polynesians, recognized that the beauty of the young men greatly surpassed that of the women. And that is precisely why their opinion is of importance to me and why I agree with them, not as a puritan but as an artist, that modesty is becoming to women and that some form of covering suits them—'*quod decet.*' "

"Well then, what is the significance of what you were telling me just now? That argument in favor of the elegance of the fair sex, which seemed to me so pertinent."

"I was going to explore the possibilities of this line of reasoning: when the female made the choice, or exercised, so to speak, the power of selection, then we saw selection working in favor of the male. Conversely no doubt it works in favor of the woman, when as at present it is the male who makes the choice."

"Hence the triumph of feminine elegance. Yes, that is as I had understood it."

"We have been in such haste, that I have not been able to pursue my ideas further. I was going to draw your attention to the fact that, whereas amongst animals the efflorescence of the male can only be transmitted to the male, *women however certainly transmit most of their characters, including beauty,*

104

to their offspring of both sexes (the phrase is from Darwin[3]). So that the strongest men, by choosing the most beautiful wives, are working for the beauty of the race, but not more for the beauty of their daughters than of their sons."

"You, in your turn, must be careful of reasoning in this way; otherwise, the more you depreciate women's beauty in favor of masculine beauty, the more you will be showing the triumph of that instinct, which still makes her beauty preferable to me."

"Or the greater the expediency of ornament and dress."

"Ornament is no more than a spice. As for dress, it can amuse for a short while and can excite desire by postponing a more complete revelation. . . . If you are not susceptible to feminine beauty, so much the worse for you, and I feel sorry for you; but don't go trying to convince me of general æsthetic laws based on a sentiment which, despite all you can say, will always remain a queer sentiment."

III

Is it then due to a 'queer sentiment' that Greek sculpture, to which we must return each time we discuss beauty, shows the man naked and the woman shrouded? Rather than recognize purely æsthetic reasons for the almost constant preference of Greek art for the figures of boys and young men and for the obstinate shrouding of the woman's body, do you prefer to see it, like de Gourmont, as 'the product of the most annoying of sexual aberrations'?"

"And what if I did choose to see it as that? Would you try and teach me the extent of the ravages of homosexuality in Greece? Besides, was it not simply to flatter the vicious inclinations of a few debauched patrons that these boys were chosen as models? And is it not open to doubt, whether the sculptor was yielding to his own artistic instincts or to the tastes of those he served? After all, it is impossible for us today to take into proper account the various requirements and conventions which constrained the artist at the time and which determined his choice, for example, at the time of the Olympic games—conventions which no doubt also obliged Michelangelo to paint not women, but naked boys on the ceiling of the Sistine Chapel, out of respect for the sanctity of the place, and precisely in order not to arouse our desires. Because, if like Rousseau, one were to hold art partially responsible for the extraordinary corruption of Greek morals . . ."

"Or Florentine. For it is remarkable that each renaissance or period of great artistic activity, in whatever country it occurs, is always accompanied by a great outbreak of homosexuality."

"An outbreak of all the passions, you should say."

"And when the day comes to write a history of homosexuality in relation to the plastic arts, it will be seen to flourish not during the periods of decadence, but, on the contrary, during those glorious, healthy periods, when art is most spontaneous and least artificial. Conversely, it seems to me that, not always, but often, the glorification of woman in the plastic arts is a symptom of decadence; in the same way that in different countries where convention required the women's rôles in the theatre to be played by boys, we see the decadence of dramatic art beginning from the time when those boys are replaced by women."

"You are deliberately confusing cause and effect. Decadence began from the day when serious dramatic art set out to please the senses rather than the spirit. It was then, as a means of attraction, that women were introduced onto the stage, and you will never remove them from it. But let us come back to the plastic arts. I have just thought of Giorgione's wonderful 'Concert Champêtre' (which I hope you do not consider a work of decadence), which as you know depicts two naked women with two young musicians fully clothed, grouped together in a park."

"From a plastic, or at least a linear point of view, no one would dare claim that the bodies of these women are beautiful. As Stevenson said they are 'too fat!' But what coloring! what deep, glowing, luminous softness! Could we not say, that whereas masculine beauty is supreme in sculpture, the flesh of women, on the other hand, lends itself best to treatment in color? Looking at this picture, I thought, here indeed is the very antithesis of ancient art: the young men clothed and the women naked; no doubt there was a dearth of sculpture in the land which produced such a masterpiece."

"And a dearth of homosexuality!"

"Oh! on that score, a small picture by Titian makes me hesitate."

"What picture?"

" 'The Council of Thirty' which shows right in the foreground, although set to one side in shadow, groups of nobles—two here, two there—in postures which leave little room for doubt. Maybe one has to see this as a sort of licentious reaction against what you just called 'the sanctity of the place.' But certainly some of the contemporary memoirs would lead one to believe that these habits had become so common that no more offense was taken at the figures of these noblemen than at the halberdiers who stand beside them."

"I have looked at that picture twenty times, without noticing anything abnormal."

"Each of us notices only what interests him. But I will say that here and there, in this picture and in these Venetian chronicles, for example, homosexuality does not seem to me spontaneous; it seems bravado, an exceptional and vicious amusement for the debauched and blasé. And I cannot help thinking that in a similar way Venetian art, so far from being popular and spontaneous, or springing vigorously from the very soil itself and from the people, as in Greece and Florence, was, as Taine said, 'complementary to the surrounding luxury,' and was a form

109

of pleasure for the nobility, like that of the French Renaissance under Francis I, which was so effeminate and so dearly bought from Italy."

"Try to disentangle your ideas."

IV

Yes, I believe that the idealization of woman is the symptom of a form of art less natural and indigenous than that presented to us during the great periods of homosexual art. In the same way that I believe, and here you must excuse my temerity, that homosexuality in both sexes is more naive and spontaneous than heterosexuality."

"It is not difficult to proceed quickly," I said, shrugging my shoulders, "if one does not care whether one is followed."

But without listening, he continued:

"This is what Barrès understood so clearly, when, wishing in *Bérénice* to depict a creature of instinct, close to nature, he made her a lesbian and the friend of 'Bougie Rose.' It was only by *education* that he succeeded in training her to heterosexual love."

"You are ascribing to Maurice Barrès hidden intentions which he did not have."

" 'Of which perhaps he did not foresee the consequences,' is all you are entitled to say; for you know quite well that in Barrès' first books the emotion itself is intentional. *For me, Bérénice represents,* he says dogmatically, *the mysterious force and impulse of the world.* A few lines further on, I even came across a subtle intuition and definition of her anagenetic rôle, when he speaks of *the serenity of her function, which is to bring to life everything which enters her;* a function he compares and contrasts with her catagenetic 'agitation of spirit.' "

Barrès' book was not sufficiently fresh in my memory for me to discuss it. But already he was continuing:

"I would be curious to know whether Barrès was aware of an opinion of Goethe's on homosexuality, which bears a close resemblance to his own views and which was reported by the Chancellor Müller (April, 1830). Let me read it to you:

"*Goethe entwickelte, wie diese Verirrung eigentlich daher komme, dass, nach rein aesthetischem Masstab, der Mann weit schöner, vorzüglicher, vollendeter als die Frau sei.*"

"Your pronunciation is so bad that I can hardly understand. Will you please translate it?"

"Goethe explained to us how this aberration actually arose from the fact that, from a purely æsthetic point of view, man was far more beautiful and more perfectly constituted than woman."

"That has nothing to do with the quotation you gave me from Barrès," I exclaimed impatiently.

"Wait a minute; we are coming to the connection: *Such a sentiment, once aroused, easily turns into bestiality. Homosexuality is as old as humanity itself, and one can therefore say that it is natural, that it resides in Nature* (*die Knabenliebe sei so alt wie die Menschheit, und man konne daher sagen, sie liege in der Natur, ob sie gleich gegen die Natur sei*). *What culture has gained at the expense of Nature will not be surrendered or given up at any price* (*was die Kultur der Natur abgewonnen habe, werde man nicht wieder fahren lassen; es um keinen Preis aufgeben*)."

"Possibly homosexual habits are so deeply ingrained in the German race that to certain Germans they appear quite natural (as the recent scandals in that country would lead us to suppose); but to a truly French mind, this theory of Goethe's remains absolutely staggering."

"Since you choose to introduce the question of ethnics, let me read you a few lines from Diodorus Siculus,[4] who, to the best of my knowledge, was one of the first writers to give us information about our ancestors' habits: *Although their women are pleasant,* he said of the Celts, *they have little to do with them whereas they show an extraordinary passion for male company. It is their custom to sleep stretched on animal skins which cover the ground, with a bedfellow on either side.*"

"Is it not clearly his intention to discredit those whom the Greeks considered barbarians?"

"At that time these habits were not considered discreditable. Aristotle also makes an incidental reference to the Celts in his *Politics.* After complaining that Lycurgus had neglected the laws pertaining to women, he said that this led to great abuses, *particularly in cases where men have allowed themselves to become dominated by women, which is a usual tendency in energetic and warlike races. I make an exception however of the Celts and of certain other nations where honor is openly paid to masculine love.*" [5]

"If what these Greeks say is true, then you must admit that we have come a long way."

"Yes, we have become somewhat cultured; that is precisely what Goethe says."

"And therefore you ask me to consider, with him, the homosexual as a backward and uncivilized . . ."

"Not necessarily; but to consider homosexuality as a very fundamental and naive instinct."

"Which would certainly provide some excuse for the fact that the inspiration of Greek and Latin bucolic verse was so frequently homosexual; verse which attempted, more or less artificially, to revive the simple modes of Arcady." [6]

"Bucolic verse started to be artificial from the time the poet ceased genuinely to love the shepherd. But no doubt one must also see it, like Oriental, Arab and Persian poetry, as one of the consequences of the position created for women, which it will be important to examine; a question of convenience . . . Of Goethe's words, I would like above all to stress the admission they make concerning culture, or rather let us say: concerning apprenticeship in heterosexuality. It may in fact be natural for the young human or the primitive human to seek vaguely contact and caresses, rather than precisely coitus; and for some, or even many people to be more disconcerted and repelled by the mystery of another sex, now that the attraction of smell is no longer there to guide them. (You see that I have dropped the argument about inferior beauty, because I do not think that sexual attraction need necessarily depend on it.) No doubt certain people will be irresistibly attracted by one sex rather than the other, as Aristophanes explains in Plato's *Symposium,* but I maintain that even the man who is exclusively attracted by the opposite sex will have considerable difficulty, when left entirely to his own devices, in daring to make the precise gesture; he will not always know how to invent it and will at first show considerable awkwardness."

"Love has always guided the lover."

"A blind guide. And since you have introduced the word 'love,' which I still wanted to keep in abeyance, I will add: that the more a man is in love, the more awkward he will be; yes, the more his physical desire is accompanied by real love, for since his desire is no longer entirely egotistical, he will be afraid of hurting the person he loves. And so long as he receives no instruction, by observing some example, of animals perhaps, or from some lesson, or from some preliminary initiation, perhaps by the woman herself . . ."

"Good God! as though a man did not find sufficient response in the reciprocal desires of the woman he loved!"

"I am no more convinced of that than Longus was. Do you remember the hesitations and mistakes of Daphnis? Doesn't he need, this great clumsy lover, an experienced woman to instruct him?"

"The clumsiness and hesitation you refer to were

surely introduced to furnish this otherwise barren novel with a little suspense and excitement?"

"Oh no! for beneath the thin veneer of affectations, I can recognize in this wonderful book, the profound science of what de Gourmont calls the Anatomy of Love, and I maintain that the story of Daphnis and Chloë is a perfect example of naturalism."

"What do you claim to have established by this?"

"That rustic lovers, not instructed by Theocritus, behaved more naively; that 'the instinct' is often insufficient to resolve the enigma of the opposite sex; practical application is necessary. A simple commentary on Goethe's words . . .

"And that is why, in Virgil, we see Damoetas sitting beneath the willows weeping for the loss of Galatea, while Menalchus takes pleasure in the company of Amyntas without reticence.

"*At mihi sese offert ultro, meus ignis, Amyntas.*

"*When the lover is close to his friend*, Leonardo da Vinci remarked, *he is in repose.*"

"If heterosexuality requires some tuition, then you must admit that today in town and country there is no lack of teachers more precociously enlightened than Daphnis."

"Whereas nowadays even in the country (or one

117

might say particularly in the country), homosexual activity is fairly rare and is considered fairly disreputable. Yes, this is what we were saying the day before yesterday; that our laws and conventions all conspire to drive one sex towards the other. There is an open, or secret, conspiracy to make a boy believe, even before his desires are awakened, that all pleasure is to be experienced with women, and that without them there can be no pleasure at all. The 'fair sex's' attractions are exaggerated to the point of absurdity; as opposed to the systematic effacement, distortion and ridicule of the masculine. Against this, however, certain artistic people will revolt; people whose sense of form we have seen to be greater than their concern for convention, at some of the finest and most admired periods of history."

"I have already answered you on that point."

"By agreeing with Perrier, if I remember correctly, and expressing your admiration for woman's concern with self-adornment, whereby she attempts, at all times and in all places, to arouse man's desires, and so supplement the inadequacy of her beauty."

"Yes; what you call 'artificial attraction.' What have you been able to prove? That adornment is becoming to women. Excellent progress! There is nothing more unpleasant than a man who overdresses or who paints his face."

118

"Once again, a boy's beauty has nothing to do with paint. In Greek sculpture we have seen how superb it is when naked. But before condemning out of hand, you should make some allowance for Western conventions; for you cannot ignore the fact that the Orientals, amongst others, do not always share our opinions.[7] Simply try dressing a boy up, offsetting his beauty instead of concealing it, and you may be able to judge the result by this passage from Montesquieu:

"*In Rome women do not appear on the stage; castrati dressed as women are used instead. This has a very bad effect on morality; because there is nothing, that I know of, which does more to inspire Socratic love amongst the people of Rome.* And further on: *During my time at Rome there were, at the Capranica theatre, two little castrati, Mariotti and Chiostra, dressed as women, who were the most beautiful creatures I have ever seen in my life, and who would have inspired the tastes of Gomorrah in people least prone to this form of depravity.*

"*A young Englishman, believing that one of them was a woman, fell madly in love with him and for more than a month remained the victim of this passion. Formerly in Florence the Grand Duke Cosimo III, out of infatuation, drew a similar inference. Imagine the effect this must have produced in Florence, which was in this respect the new Athens!* (*Voyages* I. pp. 220 and 221). And he goes on to quote in this connection the words of Horace, 'drive out what is natural and it returns at the gallop': *Naturam expelles furca, tamen usque recurret,* which we can interpret as we like."

"Now I begin to understand you properly. The 'natural' for you is homosexuality, and what humanity still has the impertinence to consider the natural and normal relationship, as between man and woman, is regarded by you as the artificial. Now, have the courage to admit it!"

He was silent for a moment and then said:

"Of course it is easy to reduce my ideas to absurdity; but when in my book they are allowed to develop quite naturally from the premises we established earlier, I don't think they will appear so ridiculous."

I then asked him to return to the subject of his book, which we seemed to have lost sight of for too long. He continued.

V

Yesterday I tried to show you that the dictates of the 'sexual instinct' were far less compelling and precise in animals than people usually choose to believe. Then, from the divers meanings loosely contained in the phrase 'sexual instinct,' I attempted to disentangle the various elements: the sheer urgency of the organ itself, the variability of taste, and the reaction to an outside influence (the object of the instinct). I discovered that the different tendencies of this complex instinct were only compact and firmly welded together, at the single instant when the smell of ovulation guided the male and drove him to coitus.

"Today I observed that men's senses were not dominated by smell and that women, possessing no overwhelming power of persuasion (I mean the irresistible and momentary attraction of animals), can only claim to be *constantly* attractive, and that they wisely apply themselves to this end with the approval, encouragement and assistance (at any rate in our Western countries) of law, convention, etc. I observed that artifice and dissimulation (the noble form of which is modesty), that decoration and dress often come to the assistance of inadequate attraction. . . . Is this to say that certain men would not be irresistibly attracted to women (or to one woman in particular) when stripped of finery? Certainly not! As we see that others, despite all the solicitations of the fair sex, the prescribed codes and the danger, still remain irresistibly attracted by boys. But I do maintain that in most cases the desire which awakens in the adolescent has no very precise urgency; that he experiences pleasure in whatever form it is offered, no matter by which sex, and that he owes his habits more to outside influences than to the promptings of his own desires. Or, if you prefer, I can put it this way: that desire rarely acquires precision on its own account and without the assistance of experience. It is rare for the first experiences to be dictated entirely by desire, even though they may be what desire itself would have chosen. There is no vocation more easily corrupted than the sexual and . . ."

"So what? For I see the point you have reached. You are suggesting that if the adolescent were left entirely to himself, without the interference of moral upbraidings—or if, so to speak, civilization grew more lax—homosexuals would be even more numerous than they are.

"It is my turn to quote Goethe's words: *The victory that culture has gained at the expense of Nature must not be surrendered or given up at any price.*"

FOURTH DIALOGUE

I

A book appeared recently," he said, "which created a certain amount of scandal. (And I have to admit that I myself could not avoid feeling a shock of disapproval as I read it.) Perhaps you know it?"

Corydon then handed me the tract on *Marriage* by Léon Blum.

"It amuses me," I said, "to hear you in your turn speak of disapproval. Yes, I have read the book. I think it is clever, and for that reason rather dangerous. The Jews are past masters in the art of debunking our most cherished institutions, those in fact which constitute the very pillars and foundations of Western civilization; in favor of I know not what license and laxity of morals, which fortunately are repugnant to our good sense and our Latin instinct for proper social values. I have always thought that this was

127

perhaps the most characteristic trait of their literature and of their theatre in particular."

"People have protested against this book," he
went on, "but no one has refuted it."

"Protests are quite enough."

"But still the problem remains, and to dodge it
is not to solve it—however indignant one feels at the
solution offered by Blum."

"What problem?"

"It is directly connected with what I was saying
the day before yesterday: the male has far more ex-
pendable sexual energy than is actually required to
meet the demands of the reproductive function of
the opposite sex and to ensure the reproduction of
the species. The sexual activity prompted by Nature
is difficult to regulate and runs the risk of preju-
dicing the good order of society, such as is understood by Western peoples."

"Hence the nostalgia for the harem in Blum's
book, which, as I have said, is repugnant to our
moral sense and our Western institutions, which
are essentially monogamous." [1]

"We prefer brothels."

"Shut up!"

"Then let's say: prostitution or adultery. There
is no getting away from it . . . unless one argues as
the great Malthus did: *that chastity is not, as some*

people suppose, an enforced virtue: it is founded on Nature and reason; in fact this virtue is the only legitimate way of avoiding the vices and misery which the law of population engenders."

"Evidently, therefore, chastity is a virtue."

"Which it is best not to try and control too much by legislation, don't you think? In my book I would prefer not to have recourse to virtue, except as a last resort. Léon Blum, who makes no appeal to virtue, but who seeks a solution that will cause the minimum of social inconvenience, is indignant at the state of affairs where the licensed prostitute is degraded, with the connivance of the law. I think that we can sympathize with him here."

"Leaving out of account the danger to public health, which occurs as soon as prostitution escapes the disgusting supervision of the State."

"That is why Blum proposes that our restless, excessive sexual energy should be directed to young women, and by that I mean honest young women, who will soon be wives and mothers."

"Yes, I remember that struck me as being particularly monstrous, and made me doubt whether he had ever moved in real French society or only amongst Levantines."

"I can certainly imagine more than one Catholic hesitating to marry a girl who had received her initiation from a Jew. But if you object to every solution offered . . ."

"Then tell me yours. I already have an unpleasant presentiment of what it is."

"I did not invent it. It is the same one that was approved in Greece."

"Oh, my God! here we are."

"Please listen to me calmly. I cannot help hoping that people with the same background and education must be able to understand each other's point of view to some extent, in spite of differences in temperament. From earliest childhood you have been educated as I have. You have been taught to venerate Greece, to which we are the heirs. In our schools and our museums, Greek works occupy the places of honor. We are asked to recognize them for what they are: human miracles of harmony, proportion, balance and wisdom. They are held up to us as examples. Besides which, we are taught that the work of art is never an accidental phenomenon, and that we must look for its explanation and motive in the people themselves and in the artist who produces it—the artist, who is only giving expression to the harmony that has first been realized within himself."

"We know all that. Go on."

"We know also that it was not only in the plastic arts that Greece excelled, but that this same perection, this wonderful gift for harmony are found in all other manifestations of its life. A Sophocles, a Pindar, an Aristophanes, a Socrates, a Miltiades, a Themistocles or a Plato are representatives of Greece no less to be admired than a Lysippus or a Phidias. This equilibrium, which we admire in each artist and in each work of art, belongs to Greece in its entirety—a beautiful plant without blemish; the full development of each branch doing nothing to hinder the development of any other."

"All this has been agreed on long ago, but it has nothing to do with . . ."

"What? Do you refuse to recognize any direct connection between the flower and the plant that bears it; between the essential quality of its sap and its behavior and formation? Will you try and persuade me that a people which was capable of offering the world such a picture of wisdom, strength, grace and happiness did not know how to conduct its own affairs—did not know first of all how to apply this wisdom and harmony to its own life and to the ordering of its morals? Yet as soon as Greek morals are mentioned, they are deplored; and since they cannot be ignored, they are turned from in horror.[2] One does not understand or one pretends not to understand. No one wants to admit that they form an integral part of the whole, that they are indispensable to the working of the social organism, and that, with-out them, the beautiful flower that one admires would be different or would not exist at all.[3]

"If, leaving aside general considerations, we examine one particular case, that of Epaminondas, for example—whom Cicero considered the greatest man produced by Greece—'and one cannot deny,' wrote one of his biographers (Walckenaer), 'that he offers one of the most perfect examples of the great leader, patriot, and sage'—then this same biographer finds it necessary to add: 'Unfortunately it seems all too certain that Epaminondas was addicted to that infamous taste, which the Greeks and particularly the Bœotians and Lacedæmonians (that is to say the most courageous) did not consider shameful' [4] (*Biographie Universelle*)."

"You must admit, however, that this type of morality occupies only a small place in Greek literature."

"Yes, in the part that has survived, maybe. But you must also remember that whenever Plutarch and Plato speak of love, they are referring to homosexual love as much as to the other.[5] Then again you have to consider the fact (and even if the observation has been made before, I do not think much importance has been attached to it) that almost all the ancient manuscripts, from which our knowledge of Greece is derived, have passed through the hands of the church. It would be interesting to make a study of the history of ancient manuscripts. One might discover perhaps whether the monastic scholars, who transcribed the texts for us, did not on occasions suppress the passages which shocked them, out of respect for their cause; or at any rate preferred to select those passages which shocked them least. Think of the number of plays by Aeschylus and Sophocles. Out of ninety plays by the one, and a hundred and twenty by the other, we are acquainted with only seven. But we do know that the *Myrmidons* of Aeschylus, for example, spoke of Achilles' love for Patroclus, and even the few verses quoted by Plutarch are sufficient to indicate the nature of their relationship. But let us go on. I am quite willing to believe that homosexual love occupied no greater place in Greek tragedy than in Marlowe's plays, for example (which in itself would be conclusive enough). What would this prove, except that drama is to be found elsewhere? Or, to express myself more clearly: that the material of tragedy is not to be found in this happy form of love.[6] Whereas, one comes across it constantly in lyric poetry, the mythological stories and all the biographies and treatises—despite the fact that almost all of them have passed through the same process of expurgation."

133

"I don't know what answer to give you. I am not sufficiently well informed."

"Anyway this is not the point which principally concerns me. For, after all, what is a Hylas, a Bathyllus or a Ganymede compared with the wonderful figures of Andromache, Iphigenia, Alcestis, Antigone, presented to us in the tragedies? I claim that we also owe this pure conception of womanhood to homosexuality, and I do not think I am going too far when I say that the same is true of Shakespeare."

"If that is not a paradox, then I would like to know . . ."

"Oh! you will quickly appreciate my point, if you will consider the fact that, given our moral outlook, no other literature has devoted more attention to adultery than the French—not to speak of all the semi-virgins and all the semi-prostitutes. The Greeks advocated an outlet which seemed natural to them, but which fills you with such indignation that you wish to suppress it. In which case, you must make men into saints; for otherwise physical desire will cause them to misuse their wives or defile young women. . . . The Greek girl was brought up with a view to maternity rather than love. Men's desires, as we have seen, were directed elsewhere; for nothing seemed more essential to the State, or worthy of greater respect, than the undefiled peace of the woman's home."

"So, according to you, it is to save the woman that the boy is sacrificed."

"We will consider in a minute whether any sacrifice was involved. But before that, I would like to answer a specious objection that has been bothering me.

"Pierre Louys reproaches Sparta for not having been able to produce any artists; and he finds occasion in this, to protest against a too austere form of virtue that was only able, he says, to produce warriors (and one that finally allowed themselves to be beaten). *The glory and grandeur of Sparta do not amount to much, for anyone who is not a blind admirer of antiquity*, wrote de Laboulaye in a note on Montesquieu. *Did anything emerge from this military monastery, except ruin and destruction? What does civilization owe to these barbarians?"* [7]

"Yes, I remember this criticism; others have made it too."

"But I am not sure whether it is just."

"Anyway the facts are there."

"In the first place you must not forget that it is to Sparta that we owe the Doric order of Paestum and the Parthenon. And again you must remember that, had the blind Homer been born in Sparta, he would have been cast into a dungeon. It is there, in the dungeons, that I imagine one must look for the artists of Lacedæmonia. Perhaps Sparta was not incapable of producing them, but since its only consideration was physical perfection, and since bodily infirmity is often the price of genius . . .".

"Yes, I see what you mean: Sparta systematically destroyed all its children who were, like Victor Hugo, born *cold, colorless and voiceless.*"

"But on the other hand it did permit Sparta to develop the most perfect physical specimens. Sparta invented selection. It is true it produced no sculptors, but it provided the model for sculptors."

"Listening to you, one would think that all the models of Athens came from Lacedæmonia, just as today the models of Rome come from Saraginesco. That is absurd. I suppose you would have me believe that all men in Greece with fine physiques were half-wits, while all the artists were bandy-legged or knock-kneed. Remember that Sophocles, as a young man, at Salamis . . ."

Corydon smiled and showed with a gesture that he granted me this point. Then he continued:

"One further remark on the subject of the Spartans. You must not overlook the fact that in Lacedæmonia homosexuality was not only admitted but, if I dare say so, was even approved. Alternatively you must not overlook the fact that the Spartans were an eminently warlike race. *The Spartans*, we read in Plutarch, *were the finest performers and the most skillful instructors in everything connected with the art of war.* In the same way you must not ignore the fact that the Thebans . . ."

"Just a minute!" I said interrupting him. "Today I have brought my own texts." And I drew from my pocket a notebook, in which the previous evening I had copied this passage from *The Spirit of Laws* (vol. IV, chapter 8) which I proceeded to read to him: "*We blush to read in Plutarch how the Thebans, in order to soften the habits of their young men, established by law that kind of love which should be prohibited in all nations of the world.*"

"Yes, that is exactly what I was telling you," he replied. "Today there is no one who does not condemn it and I know it is folly to try, as an isolated individual, to be wise;[8] but since you drive me to it, let's reread in full the passage from Plutarch, which made Montesquieu so indignant."

He fetched an old and heavy volume, opened it at the *Life of Pelopidas* and read:

"*In all the battles fought by the Lacedæmonians, either against the Greeks or against the barbarians, no one ever remembered their being*

137

defeated by an enemy inferior in numbers or even equal in numbers (as had just occurred at Tegyra, the battle which Plutarch has been describing) . . . *This battle was the first to teach the Greeks that brave and warlike men could be bred, not only on the banks of the Eurotas, but anywhere where young men shunned disgrace, proved their courage by valiant deeds, and preferred death to dishonor; here also men were found to be formidable opponents for their enemies.*"

"Well, I did not make him say it: 'anywhere where young men shunned disgrace and preferred death to dishonor.' "

"I am afraid you have misunderstood," Corydon answered gravely. "The inference one must draw from this passage is, on the contrary, that homosexuality was not considered at all reprehensible. This is borne out by all that follows." He continued reading:

"*The sacred band of Thebans was organized, it is said, by Gorgidas and was composed of three hundred chosen men. The State provided for the expenses of their training and maintenance . . . There are some who claim that this battalion was composed of lovers, and they quote in this connection the words of Pammenis: The lovers must be ranged close to one another, for to break and scatter*

138

a battalion, formed of men who loved each other, would be impossible; because those who composed it would face all dangers, some through attachment to the persons they loved and others through fear of disgracing themselves in the eyes of their lovers. That will make you realize," said Corydon, "what the idea of dishonor meant to them. *In this there is nothing astonishing,* Plutarch continues wisely, *if it be true that men are more afraid of those who love them, even when absent, than they are of all others, present. . . .* Tell me if that is not admirable?"

"Obviously," I retorted; "but it is equally true when there is no question of immoral relationships . . ."

"*And so, one of these warriors,*" he continued reading, "*struck down and seeing himself on the point of death, begs and implores his enemy to plunge the sword through his breast: 'So that at least my lover' he says, 'shall not suffer the shame, on finding my body, of seeing I was struck from behind.'* It is also related how Iolaus, loved by Hercules, shared his labors and fought by his side. (But no doubt you prefer to imagine Hercules with Omphale or Dejaneira?) Aristotle records how pairs of lovers, even in his day, would go to the tomb of Iolaus to make their vows. So it is reasonable to suppose that this battalion was named the 'Sacred Band' for the same reason that prompted Plato to define a lover as a friend in whom one felt something divine.

"The sacred band of Thebans remained invincible till the battle of Chæronea. When touring the scene of carnage after the battle, Philip halted at the spot where the three hundred lay. It was a tangled heap of bodies and weapons, and each man had his breast pierced with a sword thrust. In surprise he contemplated this spectacle, and learning that it was the battalion of lovers, he wept for them and cried: 'Let any man perish miserably, who dares suggest that these men were capable of committing or enduring anything dishonorable."

"You can say what you like," I exclaimed, "but you will never succeed in making me think of these heroes as debauchees."

"Who is trying to say that they were? Why are you so reluctant to admit that this form of love, like any other, may be capable of self-denial, self-sacrifice and sometimes even chastity? [9] The remainder of Plutarch's writing clearly shows that although it often entailed chastity, that nevertheless was not one of its pretenses.

"In support of this you know that I could quote many examples from the texts, not only from Plutarch, and that collected together they would constitute an entire book. Would you like them? They are at your disposal . . .

"I can think of no opinion more false, and yet more widely held, than that which considers homosexuality the unfortunate lot of effeminate races and decadent peoples and even sees it as an importation from Asia.[10] On the contrary, it was from Asia that the softened Ionic Order came to supplant the masculine architecture of the Doric style. The decadence of Athens commenced when the Greeks ceased to frequent the gymnasium, and we now know what should be understood by that. Homosexuality gave way to heterosexuality. And it is then that we see it acquire equal ascendency in the works of Euripides,[11] together with its natural corollary, misogyny."

"Why suddenly misogyny?"

"What would you expect? It is a fact and a very important fact; the converse of what I was pointing out just now."

"What was that?"

"That we owe our respect for women to homosexuality. Hence the wonderful pictures of women and girls in the plays of Sophocles and Shakespeare. And just as respect for women usually accompanies homosexuality, so we find that women are less highly

141

honored as soon as they are more generally desired. You must see that that is natural.

"You must also recognize the fact that homosexual periods, if I dare use the expression, are in no way periods of decadence. On the contrary, I do not think it would be inaccurate to say that the great periods when art flourished—the Greeks at the time of Pericles, the Romans in the century of Augustus, the English at the time of Shakespeare, the Italians at the time of the Renaissance, the French during the Renaissance and again under Louis XIII, the Persians at the time of Hafiz, etc., were the very times when homosexuality expressed itself most openly, and I would even say, officially. I would almost go so far as to say that periods and countries without homosexuality are periods and countries without art."

"Don't you think that this may be an illusion, and that perhaps these periods appear particularly homosexual to you simply because their peculiar brilliance invites us to study them more closely, and because the works to which they owe their fame reveal more clearly and more indiscreetly the passions which inspired them?"

"At last you are admitting what I first said to you: that homosexuality is widely prevalent. Well, I see your ideas have made some progress," said

Corydon smiling. "Moreover, I have never claimed that there was a recrudescence of homosexuality at these times, but only a more open admission and freer expression of it. Perhaps, however," he added after a moment, "we do have to believe in some recrudescence during periods of war. Yes, I believe that periods of martial exaltation are essentially homosexual periods, in the same way that belligerent peoples are particularly inclined to homosexuality."

He hesitated an instant and then asked abruptly:

"Have you ever asked yourself why the Napoleonic Code contains no law aimed at suppressing homosexuality?"

"Perhaps," I replied, rather disconcerted, "it is because Napoleon attached no importance to it, or because he reckoned that our instinctive repugnance would be sufficient."

"Perhaps it is also because such laws would have embarrassed some of his best generals. Reprehensible or not, these habits are so far from being softening and so close to being military that I have to admit I trembled for us at the time of those sensational trials in Germany, which even the Kaiser's vigilance could not succeed in suppressing; and even earlier at the time of Krupp's suicide. Some people in France were naive enough to see these as signs of

143

decadence, while I was quietly thinking to myself: we should beware of a people whose debauchery even is warlike and which keeps its women for the purpose of providing beautiful children."

"Allow me to suggest that, faced as we are with a disturbing decrease in the birth rate of France, this is hardly the moment to encourage, even if one could, the tendencies you advocate. Your theory is, to say the least of it, inopportune. The re-population . . ."

"What? You really believe that all those inducements to love will result in the birth of more children? You believe that all these women, with love in mind, will consent to be used just for child-bearing? You are joking!

"I say that the shameless stimulation, caused by pictures, theatres, music halls and many magazines only serves to deter women from their duties and make them perpetual mistresses, who no longer consent willingly to motherhood. I say that this, in its own way, is as dangerous to the State as the other form of indulgence, even when practiced to excess— and that the latter entails less waste and fewer excesses."

"Don't you think you are allowing your special interest in the case to carry you away?"

"And what if I am? The important thing is not to know whether I have an interest in defending this cause, but whether it is worth defending."

"So that, not content with tolerating homosexuality, you now claim to make a civic virtue of it . . ."

"Don't try and make me say absurd things. Whether lust is homo- or hetero-sexual, virtue consists in dominating it. I shall come to this in a moment. But without going so far as to claim as Lycurgus does (at least according to Plutarch) that no citizen can be really honest or useful to the Republic unless he has a friend,[12] I do nevertheless maintain that homosexuality in itself is not in the least harmful to the good order of society or of the State; quite the contrary."

"Will you deny then that homosexuality is often accompanied by certain intellectual defects, which more than one of your colleagues have pointed out? (I am referring to doctors.)"

"If you don't mind we will leave aside the inverts. The trouble is that ill-informed people confuse them with normal homosexuals. I hope you understand what I mean by 'inverts.' In any case, degenerates, and sick and obsessed people are to be found amongst heterosexuals as well. But alas! I am forced to admit that all too often amongst the others . . ."

"Amongst those you have the face to call normal homosexuals?"

"Yes . . . one can sometimes notice certain defects of character, for which I hold public opinion entirely responsible. For the same thing will always occur, when a natural instinct is systematically persecuted. Yes, it is public opinion which tends to make homosexuality a breeding ground for hypocrisy, malice and disrespect for law." [13]

"Why not have the courage to say—for crime?"

"Obviously, if you make the thing itself a crime. That is exactly what I blame convention for. Just as I hold the public censure of unmarried mothers responsible for three-quarters of the abortions."

"I grant you that, more generally speaking, these excellent conventions may be held partially responsible for a fall in the birth rate."

"You know what Balzac called these conventions?—'the hypocrisy of nations.' It is really staggering to see how on questions so serious, urgent and vital for the country, people prefer the word to the thing, the shadow to the substance, and how easily they sacrifice the entire stock and capital for the sake of the window-dressing."

"What are you getting at now?"

"Oh! I am not thinking of homosexuality any longer, but of the depopulation of France. But that is leading us too far astray . . .

"To get back to the subject, you simply must face the fact that in society, amongst those you meet

146

and visit most frequently, there are numbers of people, for whom you have the greatest respect, who are as homosexual as Epaminondas or myself. Don't expect me to name them. They all have the best reasons in the world for concealing the fact. And if you should suspect one of them of it, then you prefer to pretend not to notice, and so join in the game of hypocrisy. The exaggerated disapproval which you profess for it only serves to protect the offender, as will always occur in the case of excessive sanctions, of which Montesquieu said: *Inhuman cruelty in laws defeats its own purpose. When the penalty is beyond all reason, one is often obliged to grant impunity.*"

"Well then, what have you to complain about?"

"About the hypocrisy, the lies, the misrepresentation and the secretive behavior of a smuggler that you drive the homosexual to adopt."

"Then you would like to revert to the conventions of Greece?"

"For God's sake and for the good of the State."

"But Christianity has risen above that, thank God; cleansing and sublimating it all, strengthening the family bonds, consecrating marriage and over and above that, extolling chastity. I would like to hear your answer to that."

"Either you have not attended properly to what I have said, or you would have realized that my ideas contain nothing damaging to marriage or chastity. I can repeat the words of Malthus: *I would be distressed to say anything at all, directly or indirectly, that could be interpreted in a sense contrary to virtue.* I am not comparing homosexuality with chastity, but one strong desire, whether satisfied or not, with another. And I maintain that the peace of the home, the honor of the woman, the dignity of the family and the health of man and wife were more effectivcly safcguarded by the Greek way of life than by our own; while at the same time chastity and virtue were more nobly taught and more naturally attained. Do you think it was harder for Saint Augustine to aspire to God, for first having given his heart to a friend, whom he loved as much as he ever loved woman? Do you really consider that the children of antiquity were more prone to dissipation as the result of their homosexual upbringing, than our schoolchildren today with their heterosexual education? I think that a friend, even in the fullest Greek sense of the word, is a better influence on an adolescent than a mistress. I believe that the education in the art of love, which a woman like Mme. de Warens, for example, was able to give to the young Jean-Jacques Rousseau, was in certain respects more harmful to him than any Spartan or Theban education would have been. Yes, I believe that Rousseau would have been less neurotic and, as regards women, more . . . virile, if he had followed rather more closely the example of those heroes of Plutarch, whom he admired so much.

"Again, I am not comparing chastity with dissipation, of any kind whatsoever, but one form of impurity with another; and I doubt whether young men could reach marriage more spoiled than certain young heterosexuals of today.

"I say that if a young man falls in love with a girl, and if that love is profound, then there is a good chance of it remaining chaste and not being crossed at once by desire. This is exactly what Victor Hugo understood so clearly, when, in *Les Misérables*, he convinces us that Marius would rather have gone with a prostitute, than so much as entertain an impure thought for Cosette; and similarly Fielding, in *Tom Jones*, makes his hero tumble the innkeepers' daughters all the better, the more he is in love with Sophia. And it is this that Merteuil expresses so well in de Laclos' book, when the young Dancenis falls in love with the young Volange. But I add that, in view of marriage, it would have been better, and less risky for each of them, had their provisional pleasures been of a different kind.

"Finally, if you will allow me to compare one form of love with the other, I say that the passionate

149

attachment of an older person, or of a friend of the same age, is as often capable of self-denial as any feminine attachment. There are many examples of this, and illustrious ones.[14] But here, like Bazalgette in his translation of Whitman, you deliberately replace the word 'love' which both text and reality suggest, by the non-compromising word 'friendship.' [15] I say that this love, if it is profound, tends towards chastity[16]——but only, it goes without saying, if physical desire is reabsorbed into it, which simple friendship can never achieve—and that for the boy it can be the greatest incentive to courage, work and virtue.

"I say too that an older person is better able to take account of the troubles of an adolescent than any woman, even one expert in the art of love. Indeed I know certain boys too much addicted to solitary pleasures, for whom I consider an attachment of this kind would be the surest remedy.

"*I have seen someone who wanted to be a girl, and a beautiful girl, from the age of thirteen till the age of twenty-two—and after that to become a man,* said La Bruyère (*Des Femmes*, § 3)—setting rather high, in my opinion, the age at which the boy's heterosexual instincts become orientated. Until then his physical desires are indefinite and he remains at the mercy of outside influences and stimuli. He loves at random. He is ignorant and until the age of about eighteen he invites love, rather than knowing himself how to make love.

"If, while he is still this '*molliter juvenis*,' as Pliny says, more attractive than attracted, some older person is to fall in love with him, then I believe it is best for him that this person should be a friend of his own sex; a belief shared by that civilization which we studied two days ago and which you refuse to admire except for its shell. I think that this friend will jealously watch and guard him, and himself exalted by this love, will lead him to those marvelous heights, which can never be reached without love. If alternatively he falls into the hands of a woman, it can be disastrous for him. One has alas! all too many examples of that. But since at this tender age, he would still not know how to make love in any but the most indifferent manner, it is fortunately not natural for a woman to fall in love with him.

"For the Greeks, from thirteen to twenty-two (to take the years given by La Bruyère) was the age of devoted friendship, high aspiration and the proudest emulation. Only after that does the boy, in accordance with his own wishes, 'want to become a man'; that is to say, think of women—and marriage."

I had let him discourse to his heart's content and

had taken care not to interrupt him. When he had finished, he waited a time for some protestation from me. But without saying a word except "goodbye," I took my hat and left, convinced that in certain circumstances silence was the best reply.

APPENDICES

TO FRANÇOIS PORCHÉ

January 1928

My Dear François Porché,

It is said that you have written a courageous book.[1] I say so, too, and that your great courage has been in refusing to join the chorus of carping critics, while at the same time opposing yourself to evil. You have understood, and made others understand, that there is more to the subject you discuss than simply material for abuse, bad jokes and jeering.

With regard to this question, your whole book shows not only an unusual intelligence, but also an honesty, a sense of decency and a courtesy (particularly where I am concerned) to which I am little accustomed and to which therefore I am not insensible.

Furthermore, I could not read without deep emotion the pages in which you recall certain wartime recollections, and I would like you to know the echo that the expression of your esteem and sympathy finds in my heart.

How great was my surprise, as I continued reading, to encounter page after page almost nothing with which I did not have to agree. Throughout the book one feels that the most sincere effort has been made not to condemn without judging, and not to judge without understanding. I think it would be impossible to exercise greater intelligence on a matter of which one disapproves.

If certain objections, to what you say of me and my writings, immediately spring to mind, is this simply because my pride has been affected? I do not think so. It seems to me that in the portrait you have drawn of me, certain traits are a little magnified, others a little distorted (without however any intention of malice), and that in order to give yourself better grounds for contesting my ideas, you have sometimes exaggerated them. Finally this development which you claim to detect in my work and my character, and which is indicated by the very titles of your final chapters, this progressive boldness is really your own invention.

In this way you single out my book *The Immoralist*, but make no reference to the far more topical *Saul*, also published in 1902, but written five years earlier. Whether the play was produced or not, did not depend on me. I did what I could and Antoine with great courage nearly succeeded in helping. . . . I do not recall this in order to boast of being ahead of Proust, but because it is not in my nature to play the part in the farce of Moron, who does not come down from his tree to fight the bear, till somebody else has laid it low.

In the same way, according to you, "it was only lately" that I resolved to write my memoirs. Mutual friends will be able to confirm that this resolution, with all its consequences, was taken even before 1900; and not only the resolve to write them, but also to publish them during my lifetime. And likewise for *Corydon*.

This again is not very important, but it brings us back to less personal considerations. You make me out more erudite than I am. Generally speaking I have studied life rather than books, and a number of those you mention I have never read.[2] But after finishing yours, I reopened the *Divine Comedy* and was a little astonished to realize that in your chapter on "The Tradition of Moral Denunciation" you re-

157

fer to Boccaccio, Machiavelli and Aretino, but do not consult Dante, the great poet of Judgement.

He makes Virgil say: *"Now wait: to these courtesy is due,"* when referring to the kind of people you are concerned with—that is, if you take the generally accepted interpretation. For Dante is not specific on this point and leaves the reader to make his own suppositions as to the sin committed by those whom he presents in Canto XVI of the Inferno; a sin one can only deduce from chance evidence and from knowledge of the lives of the damned from other sources; as for example Jacopo Rusticucci who, we learn from a note of Lamennais, was married to "a savage-tempered wife, whom he left and abandoned himself to infamous debaucheries." Besides which, the preceding Canto seems also to have dealt with the same class of sinner; which is perhaps the reason why Dante remains so discreetly noncommittal. When speaking of the troop to which his master Brunetto Latini belongs, he contents himself with saying: *"medesmo peccato al mondo lerci"*—*"by one same crime on earth defiled"*; and when Dante asks him who his companions are, Ser Brunetto replies: *"In brief, know that all were clerks, and great scholars, and of great renown"*—*"li suoi compagni piu noti e piu sommi."* [3]

Mme. Espinasse-Mongenet, in her excellent

translation of the Inferno, also believes that Cantos
XV and XVI refer to "those who did violence to Nature." But when she tries to determine what distin-
guishes the troop to which Brunetto Latini belongs
from the one that follows, the translator hesitates,
and is doubtful whether it is the nature of the sin
committed. "It is also possible," she adds, "that the
souls are grouped in accordance with the professions
they followed in this world: on the one hand scholars
and men of letters (the homosexuals of Canto XV);
on the other hand warriors and statesmen (the homosexuals of Canto XVI)." In this latter troop are three
damned souls who come running to Dante: Guido
Guerra who *"In his lifetime did much with counsel
and with sword"*—and who, Mme. Espinasse adds,
was "proud, and a valiant soldier and a wise council-
lor." Then *"Tegghiaio Aldobrandini, whose words of
advice should have been accepted in the world
above"*; and a note by Mme. Espinasse adds, "a val-
orous knight, a man charming and wise, accomplished in arms and worthy of trust." Then Jacopo
Rusticucci, whom Mme. Espinasse describes as "a
valiant soldier, a wealthy and good Florentine, a man
of great political and moral sense."

Such are the homosexuals that Dante presents
to us.

And if one refuses to recognize the damned of

159

Cantos XV and XVI as the sort of sinners with whom we are concerned, being unwilling to admit that Dante could have allotted them so fine a part, then one still has to recognize the fact that Dante does not cast Sodom into Hell, but reserves it for Canto XXVI of the Purgatorio. Here there is no further room for doubt. Dante twice describes precisely the sin of these men, to whom his first words are, "*O souls, certain of having, whenever it may be, a state of peace.*" [4] And, once again, these sinful souls are those of poets of great renown at the time of Dante.

The importance that Dante attaches to these people, if judged by the place he allots them, the *cortesia* (to borrow his own word) with which he considers it fitting to speak of them, and the extraordinary indulgence he shows on their behalf, may be partially explicable perhaps by his feeling that Virgil himself, "*Tu duca, tu signor, e tu maestro*" would, on leaving him, go to rejoin this troop.[5] Unless one prefers to say that this indulgence came directly from Virgil. It surely came also from the consideration that both were forced to feel for the worthy men that composed it.

If I say all this, it is because your book does not say it. But what appears to me to be lacking above all is the chapter which you seemed to promise in the preface, a chapter which would constitute an answer

160

to that question which no one appears to have asked, although it seems unavoidable to me: What, in your opinion, is the duty of these "great men of letters" with regard to literature; I mean those who belong to this troop? Certainly they are not obliged to talk about love; but if they do, which is natural enough, should poets and novelists pretend to ignore the love "that dares not tell its name," when so often it is about the only love they know? To exclaim, "Enough of that; it's the last straw!" is all very well, but it is admitting at the same time that one prefers camouflage. Is it to their own advantage, this travesty which they implicitly recommend? For myself, I am afraid that this constant sacrifice to convention, subscribed to by more than one poet and novelist, sometimes celebrated, tends to distort their psychology and grossly misleads public opinion.

"But the risk of contagion!" you will say. "The example! . . ."

To share your fear I would have to be rather more convinced than I am:

1. that these tastes can be so easily acquired;

2. that the habits they entail are necessarily prejudicial to the individual, society or the State.

I consider nothing to be less proven.

Snobbism and fashion irritate me as much as they do you; and perhaps in this connection more than you. But I think you exaggerate their importance, just as you exaggerate the importance of the influence that I can have.

"Who will M. Gide persuade that one should prefer the green carnation to the rose?" Jerome and Jean Tharaud demanded recently. (And one knows what must be understood by these two symbolic flowers.) Who? But no one. And I cannot answer better than by asking the same question of those who accuse me of perverting people's minds.

If I am dealing with your book in this way, my dear Porché, then it is because I find myself faced for the first time with an honest adversary; I mean, one who is not blinded by preconceived indignation. And even against the reproach you make of showing off, which is perhaps directed partly at me, I protest only feebly. But you must admit that it is very difficult, in a matter where dissimulation has been so long an indispensable condition, to be frank without appearing cynical and to be natural with due simplicity.

Yours sincerely,

André Gide

REPLY OF FRANÇOIS PORCHÉ

Paris, 2 January 1929

My Dear André Gide,

In the last number of the *Nouvelle Revue Française* (1 January, 1929), I read the open letter which you addressed to me. You dated it January, 1928. But I have been familiar with part of it since the 19 December, 1927, because on that date you communicated some passages to me privately, and there is nothing in what you have added since to those fragments that I do not remember very well, since you told me them yourself, when on the afternoon of that day in December I had the pleasure of meeting you at your home in Paris.

If you publish this letter, revised and completed,

after a year of reflection, then it is apparently because the discussion which arose between us has not lost its interest. Allow me then, in turn, to reply to the various arguments that you have brought against me. All the more so because I, like you, clarify my ideas far better on paper than in conversation.

First of all I must thank you for the tribute you were kind enough to pay to my good faith in this affair. It gives me great satisfaction to say that the bonds which have attached me to you for a number of years, have been in no way weakened by our difference of opinion on one subject, admittedly a very important one, but which if left aside still leaves plenty of room for sympathetic understanding between us.

Now let me enter the discussion with that sense of freedom, which is one of the rules and one of the charms of our friendly relationship.

1. You charge me with having wrongly stated that you only lately resolved to write your memoirs. You abbreviated and set in inverted commas a sentence which was longer in my text, but which I admit was slightly ambiguous. Here it is: "The author of *If It Dies* . . . has written this book, we believe, with the sole and deliberate intention of admitting, or rather of loudly proclaiming, the peculiarities of his instinct; but it was only lately that he resolved to do so." In my opinion your tardiness was not in your

determination to write your memoirs, but in your resolve to bring certain passages of those memoirs to
the attention of the public. You tell me that from the
first, you determined to publish these memoirs during
your lifetime. I do not for a moment doubt your
word. But the fact remains that since making up your
mind (before 1900 according to you), you have de-
layed following it up for more than twenty years. We
find the same hesitation, or the same deliberate post-
ponement, when it comes to *Corydon*. Writing (and
I mean writing not simply for oneself but with the
intention of afterwards publishing) and presenting
one's writing to the public, are two quite different
things. It was the latter which principally interested
me, since I was studying the changes in public opinion with regard to this anomaly. However firm your
secret intentions may have been, they remained
none the less in suspense. Between intention and ac-
tion there is a wide gap and you did not find it easy
to make the leap. It was in this respect that I thought
I was entitled to say that during the space of twenty
years your attitude had grown progressively bolder.

2. Now it is quite possible that certain personal
considerations may have contributed to your hesi-
tancy. On page 187 of my book I alluded to these
scruples. I even added: "Reasons of an intimate nature such as this, which seem like excuses to the in-

sensible, are often the most decisive ones." You remind me of *Saul*, which was published in 1902 and which in fact I neglected to mention. According to you, *Saul* would "certainly be more topical" than the *Immoralist*. That is not my opinion. In a sense *Saul* is more explicit but, belonging to the theatre, it acquires the quality of an impersonal composition, thanks to the illusions of the stage. Furthermore the subject of the play is borrowed from the Bible. This no doubt allows the principal hero more violent sentiments and cruder expression, but at the same time it envelops them in a fabulous atmosphere, which serves as a veil. *The Immoralist* transposes nothing. It does not state, but allows itself to be understood. Whether novel or lyrical confession, this completely modern work speaks to us directly with a soft insistent voice. *The Immoralist* can disturb us; *Saul*, never.

3. I know the passage from the *Divine Comedy* to which you refer, and I have always been struck by the deference with which Dante speaks of the people "by one same crime on earth defiled." In the chapter devoted to Wilde I have recalled the place to which the poet assigns them in his Inferno; but it is true that I omitted to mention the great "courtesy" he showed towards them. Perhaps, not belonging to this troop myself, I was inclined to stress the fact that

Dante confined them to his Inferno, rather than gratefully acknowledging the politeness he extended them. One of this troop, on the contrary, writing in my place would no doubt have overlooked the damnation and stressed the kind words, which restore the prestige of this outlawed caste. But you also draw my attention to the fact that the "poet of Judgement" placed some of the souls guilty of the same error in his Purgatorio. That I admit I overlooked. But I have on no occasion taken the care to be thorough with my historical and literary references. In fact I have deliberately avoided excessive documentation, which would have involved me in another pitfall: that of furnishing unhealthy curiosities with a little encyclopedia of information. Finally, amongst those we are concerned with, there are some whom I have spoken of with the greatest possible *"cortesia."* I can not be suspected of having taken the trouble to misrepresent Dante's attitude, because its leniency was capable of restoring the prestige of those at whom I was aiming. You certainly did not say this, and I am sure you did not think it.

4. I had not read Balzac's *Vautrin*, when I wrote my book; but I have since made good my omission, after you yourself drew my attention to it at our last meeting a year ago. But I am far from sharing your high opinion of this work. Jacques Collin in the play

seemed even less revealing than in the novel. Nothing is said except by allusion, and then only with the utmost caution.

5. You ask me a serious question: should the great men of letters who belong to this troop pretend, when they talk of love, to ignore the "love that dares not tell its name," when so often it is about the only love they know?

True art does not live by deception, and I believe, as you do, that all misrepresentation puts the author in grave danger of falsifying psychology. Never have I intended to limit the rights of an author, or to restrict his duties towards the truth. I have said it before and I repeat it now. I have never reproached Proust, for example, for having created Charlus. Perhaps you will think that if I exonerate Marcel Proust for creating Charlus, it is because the ugliness of the character and the grotesqueness of the extravagancies to which he allows himself finally to be dragged are such as to give a horrible aspect to his tastes? No. I would acknowledge and admire just as well a gracious character, providing that artistic care and scrupulous observation were the only factors in its conception. If it is true, as some assert, that when Proust speaks of "Albertine," one has to understand "Albert," then it is regrettable, for this is nothing less than the substitution of one world for another. It

168

is wanting to represent green by red. And for the reader to possess the key to the stratagem is not enough to rectify the matter. Here it is the author who has fallen into his own trap, with the result that Charlus is intensely real, while Albertine remains a phantom.

Of course the work of art is free. However dangerous the exercise of this freedom may be, and whatever abuses it can lead to, it must still be safeguarded. Our very dignity depends on it.

But there is an essential difference between a work of art and a tendentious work, conceived simply for the purpose of propaganda, with a particular religious, political or moral end in view. The dividing line between the two is certainly hard to determine; in fact it is more than a line; it is a zone. Most often it is in the spirit of a work, that it will be apparent whether the dividing line has been crossed. The author himself is rarely deceived. And how should he be deceived, when it was a strong impulse which drove him to speak his mind? He knows quite well how easily his obsessive concern to exercise a direct influence can sweep away his scruples as a disinterested artist. You cannot deny that you had this desire for moral influence, and I do not think you would even try to deny it. It is your deliberate intention that I blame. What is *Corydon?* A tract.

6. For the remainder; according to you it is not proven:

1st. That these tastes can be so easily acquired;

2nd. That the morals they entail are necessarily prejudicial to the individual, society or the State.

I have nothing to add to what I said in my book. There is one point, in effect, on which I despair of convincing you. On this one point our attitudes will always differ. A certain disagreement between us will always remain unresolved. Here good faith is no longer enough to reach an understanding.

Perhaps it will strike you as being only fair to put before your readers my reply to your open letter. Of this I leave you the sole judge, and I beg you to believe me, dear André Gide,

Yours very truly,

François Porché

A letter from Benjamin Crémieux, repeating less explicitly almost the same things, insisted particularly on Dante's lack of toleration for inverts, and drew my attention to the fact that Dante placed them in the most scorching part of hell. On the other hand a correspondent from Italy reproaches me for not having noticed that in the Purgatorio the inverts are placed closest to heaven. However I am willing to agree with Benjamin Crémieux and the correspondent whose erudite letter I quote above, that Dante "gave no evidence of any particular indulgence to homosexuals," and that if he speaks of them at such length in the *Divine Comedy*, then it is simply because at that time they were known to be very numerous and to include numbers of illustrious people.

18 *January* 1929

Sir,

Your remarks, on the treatment accorded to homosexuals in the *Divine Comedy*, have interested me keenly. Allow me to make three observations on the subject, which I think tend to bear out your theory.

1. There can be no possible doubt about the nature of the offense committed by the damned of Cantos XV and XVI of the Inferno. Virgil, in point of fact, sketched the topography of Hell in Canto XI. He described the seventh circle as divided into three circlets of gradation. The blasphemers, those violent against the Deity and those violent against Nature are enclosed in the third, the smallest of these rounds, *which seals with its mark* (the rain of fire) *both Sodom and Cahors*

172

a pero lo minor giron suggella
del segno suo e Sodoma et Caorsa.

(Inferno, Canto XI, 49, 50)

We shall meet those who did violence against the Deity in Canto XIV of the Inferno.

The usurers[6] in Canto XVII. It is therefore certain that the crowds of the intermediate Cantos, the *famiglia*, the *greggia* of Canto XV, the *torma* of Canto XVI constitute the population of Sodom in hell.

2. I do not believe that Dante thought of showing courtesy towards homosexuals out of regard for his master and guide.

Whatever the case, Virgil's "place" in limbo, the first circle of the Inferno, is perfectly determined by the celebrated apostrophe *ornate l'altissimo poeta* etc., (Inferno IV) and by the less well-known passage in which Virgil gives Statius the "Literary News" of the Græco-Roman world and says to him: *We are with that Greek* (Homer) *to whom the Muses gave suck more than to any other, in the first circle of the dark prison:*

nel primo cinghio del carcere cieco.

(Purgatorio, XXII.)

As for those to whom "courtesy is due," Dante has already asked news of two of them: Tegghiaio Aldobrandini and Jacopo Rusticucci *che a ben far poser gl'ingegni* (Inferno, VI). We know also that he held them in the highest esteem.

But Dante's judgements on the living and the dead are usually subjective, partial and influenced by his feelings as a poet. He happens to distinguish the individual's theological value (his station in the after life) from his social value (the good he has been able to do his fellow citizens even though he lose his soul). The reasons for which he happens to damn or save a soul often elude us and are sometimes cleverly concealed.

So in his eyes the misfortunes of Jacopo Rusticucci were the work of a shrewish wife, who had incited him to evil (?), and had denounced and persecuted him.

La fiera moglie più ch'altro mi nuoce. (Inferno, XVI).[7]

As Rusticucci was the only one of the three damned of Canto XVI whom Dante could have known personally (leaving out of account Guglielmo Borsiere, who does not appear before verse 70), then it is not too absurd to suppose that this scene was inspired by a desire for vengeance against Rusticucci's wife (the present tense seeming to indicate that she was still alive).

A very curious example shows the quite arbitrary distinctions that the poet sometimes makes between the damned "of the same category."

Dante had known Brunetto Latini since childhood. He retained in his heart

La cara e buona imagine paterna.

It was Ser Brunetto who, day by day, taught the young Dante, *"come l'uom s'eterna."* When he refinds his master amongst the "brotherhood," the first cry of the poet is a cry of surprise, of sad surprise, *"Siete voi qui, Ser Brunetto?"* (Inferno, XV).

Later on he gives us to understand "that he has no prejudices." Only the rain of fire stops him from embracing Rusticucci and his two companions. He tells them: "Not contempt, but sorrow, your condition fixed within me, so deeply that it will not leave me soon." *Non dispetto ma doglia.* (Inferno, XVI.)

But in the presence of the teacher of his youth, of the companion of his best reading, of the man who knew how to soothe the agonies of a generous soul and the anxieties of a sensitive heart, Dante was overwhelmed; he had only the strength to murmur:

Are you here, Ser Brunetto?

Siete voi qui . . .

What conflicting thoughts and emotional tumult in those three words!

So it was true. . . . I did not believe it; I have

175

never believed it. I was told; it was repeated to me; I was given proof. I did not believe it; I did not want to believe it. I had such respect for your teaching; I valued your ideas and your conversation so much; all that came of you was so dear and precious to me, that I could not bear to hear this calumny repeated in my presence. But it was not a calumny. It was true. Because of my immense affection for you, I did not want such a thing to be true. And yet, *siete voi qui,* are you here, Ser Brunetto!

Now let us hear him speak of a homosexual that he does not like. He starts by calling him (or rather having him called) "scurf." (Inferno, XV).

Who is it? It is his priest, Andrea dei Mozzi, Bishop of Florence from 1287 (Dante was then twenty-two years old) to 1295. Boccaccio in his *commentary* tells us the story of this man: "on account of this wretchedness, in which he showed himself to be a very dishonest sinner, and on account of his other stupidities (sic) (*altre sciocchezze*) which the common people still relate, he was transferred by the Pope to the Bishopric of Vicenza, as a result of the steps taken by his brother Messer Tommaso de Mozzi, a very honorable knight, who, enjoying considerable favor with the pope, wished to remove such an abomination from his own sight and from the

176

sight of his fellow citizens." The intervention of the brother, who thought "that the scandal had lasted long enough," was dramatic, don't you think?[8] But Dante did not mind. He would not let his victim go; he pursued him from *the Arno to the Bacchigline,* and in a terrifying synthesis joined vice with death.

Ove lascio li mal protesi nervi. (Inferno, XV).

Ah! This time (and it is the third observation I intend to submit to you) one has to admit that Dante does not remain "discreetly imprecise."

At Vicenza the guilty prelate was left with "his ill-strained nerves" or "his badly balanced nervous system," as the virtuous commentators will not fail to say. Dante in point of fact says: "his nerves stretched unseasonably." Rarely, I think, has a briefer, happier and more complete definition of sexual inversion been given—or one that was more impartial.

In brief, these are my observations:

1. That the souls, met by Dante and Virgil in Cantos XV and XVI of the Inferno, were—without any possible doubt—those of inverts.

2. That Dante showed no evidence of any particular indulgence to homosexuals; but his ethical criterions did not depend on their conceptions of physical love.

3. That far from remaining "discreetly impre-

cise," the poet gave, in some ways, a clinical definition to the love "that dares not tell its name."

Please excuse, sir, this overlong letter, etc.,

Léon Kochnitzky.

COMMENTS ON
THE SECOND DIALOGUE
IN CORYDON

by Frank Beach

Although it was formulated nearly four decades ago, the major thesis of the Second Dialogue in *Corydon* is in accord with present-day interpretations of human sexual behavior. People who say that homosexual activities are biologically abnormal and unnatural are wrong. Some of the evidence that led Mr. Gide to this belief has been modified by more recent findings, but his final conclusion stands. The

179

goals of this Commentary are to bring the pertinent zoological evidence up to date, and to evaluate Mr. Gide's reasoning in the light of current theories.

One obstacle to the complete realization of these objectives arises from the absence of any clear-cut definition of homosexuality. The term means different things to different people, but the author of *Corydon* does not tell us precisely what it means to him. Instead of beginning with the uncritical assumption of a mutual understanding, it is preferable to set forth the significance of the term as used in this discussion. Homosexuality refers exclusively to overt behavior between two individuals of the same sex. The behavior must be patently sexual, involving erotic arousal and, in most instances at least, resulting in satisfaction of the sexual urge.

Why does homosexuality exist? Because, according to Gide, the sexual drive of males greatly exceeds that of females and must find some outlet; and because males are naturally and normally sexually attracted to one another. In support of this argument he cites a great deal of evidence pertaining to many animal species. Unfortunately, however, there are occasional misstatements of fact and in several instances only part of the evidence is included.

It is stated that throughout the lower orders an excess of males over females is the normal condition

180

and that many males are thereby deprived of the opportunity for heterosexual mating. The fact is that males do greatly outnumber females in a few species, but for the vast majority of animals the sex ratio is very nearly one to one. Furthermore, abortive sexual contacts between males are, so far as we know, neither more nor less common in one case than in the other. The occurrence of such behavior does not necessarily connote a specific attraction between males. It may simply reflect inability to recognize the sex of another individual. Male frogs in breeding condition will embrace a male or a female with equal readiness because they cannot distinguish the sex of a potential partner until it has been clasped. A second male is soon released and the complete spawning pattern is carried out only after a female has been found.

Gide suggests in the Second Dialogue that even when males and females are present in equal numbers homosexuality is "natural" because there is still an inequality of need. This is supposed to arise from the fact that females are only receptive for brief periods whereas males are constantly active, due to "the superabundance of the male element,—seminal material." Both statements call for modification. The amount of seminal material present in the masculine generative tract has nothing to do with sexual responsiveness or capacity. Destruction of the sperm-producing part of the sex glands and surgical removal of the associated structures in which seminal fluid is stored renders a male infertile but does not reduce his display of sexual behavior.

Nor is it generally true that males are ready and able to mate at any time although the female's sexual attractiveness and receptivity is restricted to the short time when she is susceptible to impregnation. Both males and females of most animal species are sexually inactive throughout most of the year. The majority of wild creatures have well-marked breeding seasons within the limits of which both sexes seek sexual contact. The female does not lose her stimulating value for the male as soon as she has been fertilized but often continues to accept one male after another until the season is over, after which time neither sex is interested in or capable of intercourse.

Some wild and many domestic species can breed throughout the year and in such cases the female usually comes into heat at regular intervals unless the cycle is interrupted by pregnancy. But even in these instances it is unsafe to conclude that the male's sexual capacity greatly exceeds that of the female. It is obvious that the *reproductive potential* of the male is greater, but this is because he is not charged with the responsibility of gestation and can sire more offspring than a single female can conceive and carry. There is, however, a vast difference between fertilizing a female and exhausting her erotic desire. Female monkeys are fertile for about five days in each month and during this interval one female usually cohabits with a succession of males, exhausting one consort after another until her receptive period has run its course. Females of other primate species attract the male and permit copulation at times when they are not fertile. In some apes females indulge in frequent intercourse before puberty and throughout pregnancy.

Gide's argument for homosexuality as a compensatory adjustment which relieves the male's excess sexual need is not substantiated by the zoological evidence. Is there any support for the implication that males possess a natural sexual attraction for one another? With proper qualification this question can be answered in the affirmative.

Under some circumstances male animals deliberately make sexual advances to other males. In its simplest form this behavior represents a substitute response in which a sexually aroused individual lacking opportunity for heterosexual coitus temporarily reacts to another male as he would a female. A feminine partner may be preferred, but the masculine one is accepted in the absence of an alternative. Males that are treated as females usually are unwilling participants in the relationship. Occasionally,

183

however, an animal will respond in a manner characteristic of the female. When this occurs the masculine reactions of the partner are intensified. Nevertheless, if a receptive female enters the scene at this point *both males* promptly mate with her in normal fashion. Males that adopt the feminine rôle in response to sexual aggression by another male inevitably display vigorous heterosexual behavior when given an opportunity to do so. They are, in a sense, bisexual.

Male monkeys that have formed an emotional attachment for one another sometimes engage in homosexual matings although feminine partners are available. This is something more than a substitute response and may approximate the type of homosexualty discussed in *Corydon*. In no case, however, do such alliances interfere with subsequent heterosexual activity; and never, so far as is known, are they as frequent or complete as male-female pairings.

An important point to which Gide pays very little attention is the fact that homosexuality is by no means confined to males. The love of Achilles for Patroclus is mentioned repeatedly, but no emphasis is placed upon Sappho's passion for one after another of the young heterai who attended her school. The comparative neglect of lesbianism seriously weakens the major argument in *Corydon*. It is affirmed that

184

men do not need women for sexual satisfaction, but the author appears oblivious to the fact that the converse is equally true. The explanation for this bias is obvious. Homosexuality is said to stem from an inequality of sexual needs and desires, and at the same time homosexual men also indulge in heterosexual relations. Since their limited erotic capacity is easily exhausted, women should rarely be forced to resort to homosexual alliances.

The facts are patently at odds with this thesis. It is perfectly clear that homosexuality among women is as ancient and as widespread as comparable relations between men. We see this in human history and it is also reflected in the zoological evidence. In fact the display of masculine behavior by female animals is much more common than the execution of feminine responses by males. Every animal breeder knows that under certain conditions female cattle, horses, swine, sheep, dogs and cats will mount other females and go through the male's mating pattern. And the female thus approached reacts to her like-sexed partner much as she would to a male. Very often the display of masculine behavior indicates that a female is ready to breed and if she is turned in with a male she eagerly solicits his sexual attentions and willingly receives him. The masculine, or homosexual pattern is not unnatural; instead it constitutes a normal element in the sexual repertoires of these species.

How do the facts as set forth here modify or support Gide's point of view? The question cannot be answered definitively because of his failure to provide us with a straightforward definition of what he means by homosexuality. In any event it is necessary to expand the concept so that it lays equal emphasis upon sexual relations between females as well as between males. And we must, in some arbitrary fashion, allow for different degrees of homosexuality.

As a crude approach to this type of differentiation we might postulate three hypothetical classes of individuals, recognizing that in actuality all degrees of intergradation exist. One group includes those men and women who are capable of sexual excitement and complete response only in association with other individuals of their own sex. They are exclusively homosexual and appear to be omitted from Gide's categorization, unless they are what he calls "inverts." A second class comprises males and females for whom sexual arousal and erotic satisfaction are possible only in a relationship with an opposite-sexed partner. These individuals are exclusively heterosexual. And finally there is an intermediate group with bisexual proclivities. They are capable of am-orous attachment to a partner of their own as well as the opposite sex, although it is impossible to state that they find either sex equally attractive. On the basis of the zoological evidence one might predict that bisexual human beings would outnumber the other two groups combined.

If this strictly theoretical analysis is valid, why are there so few men and women who actually behave in this fashion? The simplest reply is that the logic is faulty, that interpreting human behavior in terms of evidence pertaining to other species is not permissible, and that reactions which are natural to other creatures are not necessarily natural in man. Within limits this is undoubtedly correct. But the established facts of human evolution make it difficult to believe that behavior which appears with great regularity in all or nearly all mammals and particularly in all primates is completely aberrant in our own species. It seems much more logical to suppose that bisexual tendencies are inherent in human beings but rarely achieve overt expression because of some suppressing force.

Gide observes that all forms of sexual activity except coitus between husband and wife are generally considered socially undesirable and usually are subject to severe cultural repression. By this means natural impulses toward homosexual behavior are inhibited from childhood and may never be recognized even by the individuals possessing them. This probably is true although the strength of the underlying tendency may be emphasized unduly in *Corydon*. Some non-European cultures impose no rules against homosexuality and any individual is free to adopt the rôle of the opposite sex. In some cases the individual involved may be accorded special social rank. It is noteworthy, however, that even in the absence of prohibitions against homosexuality, heterosexual relations remain the predominant form of erotic outlet for adult members of all societies.

We find ourselves, then, agreeing with Gide in his contention that homosexual behavior should be classified as natural from the evolutionary and physiological point of view. It does not necessarily follow that the behavior is socially desirable. This is a question which cannot be answered on the basis of biological evidence. Too much depends upon the value judgments of other members of the social group, and no broad generalization can possibly be valid since attitudes change from generation to generation and from culture to culture.

We agree again with the statement that exclusive heterosexuality probably reflects social channelization of the sexual urge rather than any immutable natural law.

We differ from Gide's thesis in giving lesbianism a position of equal prominence with masculine homosexuality. And we are at variance with him in our belief that the strength of the biological forces inclining most individuals toward heterosexual relations are greater than those that tend to produce homosexual alliances.

Yale University, July, 1949

NOTES

PREFACE

1. Certain books—and those of Proust in particular—have accustomed the public to consider more calmly a subject which they previously pretended or preferred to ignore. Many people imagine that by ignoring a problem they are solving it. But I am afraid that these books have, at the same time, helped to confuse the issue. The theory of the man-woman, of the *sexuelle Zwischenstufen* (intermediate degrees of sex)—which Dr. Hirschfeld put forward in Germany some years before the war, and which Marcel Proust seems to have supported—may well be true; but it is only concerned with explaining certain types of homosexuality, which are precisely those I do not deal

193

with in this book—cases of inversion, effeminacy and sodomy. And I realize now that one of the great shortcomings of my book is that I do not deal with them at all—for they are shown to be far more frequent than I previously supposed.

Even admitting that Hirschfeld's theory of the "third sex" meets these cases, it certainly cannot explain what is usually called "Greek love," which has nothing whatsoever to do with effeminacy.

FIRST DIALOGUE

1. Of course Bazalgette has the option to choose (and the choice is forced on him by the French language) each time the *gender* of the English word is indefinite, and to translate, for example, "the friend whose embracing awakes me" as "*l'amie qui* . . . etc."—although by so doing he is deceiving both the reader and himself.

But he has no right to draw conclusions from the text after he himself has altered its meaning. He admits, with disarming candor, that Whitman's liaisons with women, to which he refers in the biography, are purely imaginary. His desire to draw his hero onto the side of heterosexuality is so great, that when he translates "the heaving sea," he finds it necessary to add "like a woman's bosom," which from a literary point of view is absurd and profoundly anti-Whitmanesque. When I read this translation, I went straight to the original text, *certain* that there must be some . . . slight error. Similarly, when we read *"mêlé à celles qui pèlent les pommes, je réclame un baiser pour chaque fruit rouge que je trouve,"* it goes without saying that the use of the feminine gender is Bazalgette's own invention. The book abounds with such examples, all of which could be attributed to Bazalgette, so that Whitman really seems to be addressing Bazalgette when he exclaims: "I am not what you suppose." The literary distortions are numerous and are important because they completely alter the sense of Whitman's poetry. I can think of few translations which betray the author more completely . . . but this is taking us too far away from our subject.

SECOND DIALOGUE

1. "If there is one vice or one ailment repulsive to French mentality, French morality, French health, it is, to speak frankly, homosexuality."

Ernest Charles,
Grande Revue
(25 July, 1910), p.399.

2. "If the nervous system is centralized, as in the case of weevils, then their enemy the cerceris gives only one stab. If movement depends on three

ganglia, then three stabs are inflicted. If there are nine ganglia, then nine stabs. The ammophilia acts in the same way when it requires the grubs of the nocturnal lepidoptera for its own grubs; if a sting in the cervical ganglion seems too dangerous, then the attacker contents itself with slow chewing, in order to achieve the necessary degree of immobility . . . etc." (for example, Remy de Gourmont *loc. cit.* page 258; on the observations of J. H. Fabre. See the excellent criticism of the mythology by Marchal, reported by Bohn, *Nouv. Psych. Animale,* pp. 101–104).

Almost the whole of this dialogue was written in the summer of 1908. Bohn's new animal psychology had not yet appeared, and I had not then come across Max Weiler's memorandum on *Modification of the Social Instincts,* 1907, the theories of which closely resemble those which I expound here.

3. At least in the so-called "superior" species.

4. Lester F. Ward, *Pure Sociology* (The Macmillan Company, 1911), part II, chap. XIV.

5. Or almost constant. At the end of this dialogue we shall consider certain species which, though appearing to be exceptions to this law, in fact confirm my theory.

6. This dimorphism is scarcely perceptible in the equine species; but what I say about it applies to all other families.

7. *Journal of Researches into the Natural History and Geology of the Countries visited during the Voyage round the world of H.M.S. Beagle under command of Captain Fitz Roy, R.N.*
(London Edition, 1901), p. 201.

8. Ibid.

9. At the end of this section we shall see that if, in certain species, the instinct acquires precision,

then immediately the proportion of the male element decreases.

10. "The males appear to be infinitely more numerous than the females, and probably not more than one per cent of them can accomplish their destiny" wrote de Gourmont in *The Anatomy of Love* after relating Blanchard's story "of the naturalist who captured a female silkworm, put it in his pocket and made his way home escorted by a cloud of more than two hundred males." See Darwin, *Descent of Man* (Selection in relation to sex). "The males of certain species can become so common that the point is reached when almost all remain celibate. With the small silver-blue cockchafers which frequent the plants of waterside spiraea and which are collected for mounting in jewelry (*Hoplia cerulea*) one finds only one female to every 800 males; with maybugs (*Rhizotrogus œstivus*) there is one female to every 300 males."

Edmond Perrier,
Le Temps (1 August, 1912).

11. Perhaps the most interesting observations on this point are those of Fabre on the Osmies, which according to him predetermine the sex of their eggs by the size of the place chosen for hatching the larvæ. In the same way bees produce either queens, drones or workers according to the dimensions of the cell they construct for the egg and the food they give to the larva. The male is the *minus habens*.

I have also made a note of the observations of W. Kurz on the *cladoc eras* (reported by Claus). "The males generally appear in the autumn; but as has recently been shown, they can appear at any time of the year because biological conditions become unfavorable as the result of modifications in their surroundings." (*Zoologie*, p. 636.) René Worms in his remarkable study of the Sex of Infants in France reaches the conclusion that, contrary to general opinion, a greater proportion of male births in a nation is an indication of poverty; that, as wealth increases, so this excess diminishes until finally, in a state of general prosperity, it gives place to an excess of female births. "It will be seen," adds Edmond Perrier whom I am quoting, "that this conclusion is in complete agreement with what I myself am advancing . . ."

Edmond Perrier,
Le Temps (1 August, 1912).

12. In the same way there is no sport of the male which, after perhaps having played its part in selection, does not free itself and become an end in itself.

I will here recall what Fabre said of the *Locustidae,* and which he could just as well have said of birds: "What purpose does this well-tuned instrument serve? I will not go so far as to deny it any rôle in mating. But that is not its fundamental function. Above all the insect uses it to express its joy of living, and to sing of the happiness of existence. . . ."

13. "Here, *as always with animals,* mating only takes place when the female is in rut. Otherwise she will not tolerate the approach of the male."

Samson,

Zootechnie (*Luttes des ovides*), II, 181.

14. "The sexual instinct in the male is aroused at all times by the odor exuded by the female in rut; in the female it normally only displays itself at fixed periods and under the intrinsic influence of the work-

ing of ovulation, her own ovaries being the control-ling factor. Furthermore, when she has been fecun-dated, this instinct is dormant during the whole period of gestation and during part of the period of suckling, which with most of our domestic animals amounts to about a year."

Samson, II, 87.

15. ". . . a greater activity of the vaginal glands, the secretion of which gives out a particular odor, which the male's sense of smell forces him to recognize."

Samson, V, 181, 182.

16. Let us quote an example from Fabre. One female of the small night emperor moth will at-tract a host of male emperor moths into Fabre's study. These moths beseige the trellis-work cover in which the female is encaged; while she, perched on a twig that Fabre has hung in the middle of the cage, remains indifferent. If next day Fabre moves the female to a new cage and a new perch, the males

still flock to the first cage left at the far end of the room and cluster round the old perch which is impregnated with subtle emanations. However apparent the female is to them (and Fabre takes care to place her on their direct route), they pass straight by and hurl themselves at the old perch; then when they have knocked it to the floor, they cluster round the spot on the chair where it had been standing.

17. A bitch that I know gets along well with two cats. When the female cat is in heat she grows very excited and sometimes tries to mount her like a tomcat.

18. "One even sees cows in season trying to mount each other; whether their idea is to try and provoke the male, or whether the visual representation, which they conjure of the desired act, obliges them to try and copy it," wrote de Gourmont, after saying a few lines earlier that "in general, animal aberrations require quite a simple explanation." He then adds: "It is a marvelous example of the motive

force of images, because it is so absurd." I am afraid it is more absurd than marvelous.

Physique de L'amour (Anatomy
of Love), pp. 229, 230.

19. "One also sees certain other animals giving themselves to the love of males of their own sex," Montaigne rather strangely remarks in *L'Apologie de Raimond Sebond.*

20. Even de Gourmont knows that "under normal conditions the female must stop giving out her sexual odor immediately after intercourse."

Physique de L'amour (Anatomy of Love).

21. These things have been so frequently observed that even in Béleze's out-of-date *Dictionary of Practical Life* we find the following in the article on Pigeons: "It sometimes happens that the nest, which should consist of a couple (?), consists of two males or two females. One perceives the presence of

204

two females because they lay two sets of eggs; and the presence of two males because they disturb the pigeon house." (?)

22. "The same rhythmical movements of the body and the same lateral flagellations are frequently used between males. Whilst the one on top agitates itself and vigorously moves its front legs, the one beneath remains still. Sometimes a third crazy animal and even a fourth will arrive and climb on the others. The topmost makes rhythmical movements and vigorously beats its front legs; the others remain motionless. And so for a while the rejected creatures deceive themselves."

J. H. Fabre (*Cerocomes*), vol. III, 272.

Has this patient observer, Fabre, really observed whether it is after *rejection* by the female that these homosexual activities take place? Is it only because they have been refused that these males copulate with one another? Or do they do it before there is any question of rejection?

23. What observations could appear more un-prejudiced, more honest than those of the pains-taking Fabre on the cerceris? observations com-pletely invalidated, or at least reversed, today by Marchal.

24. Or the proportion of male element—that is to say a superabundance of seminal material, since the individual does not achieve in coitus the purpose of its life.

25. It is a remarkable fact that, precisely in this species (*Mantis religiosa*) and despite the small number of males, each female displays an inordinate greed. Even after fecundation she still offers herself for coitus and remains attractive to the male. Fabre relates how he saw one of them secure and then de-vour seven males in succession. The sexual instinct, which we here see to be compelling and precise, has exceeded its purpose. I naturally came to ask myself whether in such a species where the number of males is proportionately inferior, where consequently the

instinct is more precise and where therefore no un-employed material remains on which the catagenetic force can operate, no "material for variation"—whether under such circumstances, dimorphism does not operate in favor of the female—or to put it otherwise: whether the males of this species are not *less* brilliant in appearance than the females. And this is precisely what we do discover to be the case with the praying mantis, the male of which is "frail, drab, undersized and miserable" (to borrow Fabre's adjectives) and which can never aspire to that "dazzling exhibition" in which the female spreads her extraordinarily beautiful wings, transparent and fringed with green. Fabre, however, makes no observation whatsoever on this singular reversal of attributes, which here corroborates my theory. These considerations, which I relegate to a footnote because they break away from my main line of reasoning and which in consequence I fear may pass unnoticed, seem to me nevertheless to be of the greatest interest. Having pushed this new and admittedly daring theory to its logical conclusions, the joy I experienced on discovering an example to confirm it coming, so to speak, to meet me, was only comparable to the joy of Edgar Allan Poe's treasure hunter, who unearthed the casket full of jewels, in the exact spot to which his calculations had led him. . . . Perhaps one day I shall publish fuller observations on this subject.

THIRD DIALOGUE

1. A similar naivete is shown by Addison in a passage I have taken from *The Spectator* (No. 265).

"It is observed among birds, that nature has lavished all her ornaments upon the male, who very often appears in a most beautiful head dress: whether it be a crest, a comb, a tuft of feathers, or a natural little plume, erected like a kind of pinnacle on the very top of the head. As nature, on the contrary, has poured out her charms in the greatest abundance on the female part of our species, so they are very assiduous in bestowing upon themselves the finest garniture of art. The peacock in all his pride does not display half the colours that appear in the garment of a British Lady, when she is dressed either for a ball or a birthday . . ."

Or should this be treated as irony?

2. "The custom of wearing a white or scarlet flower in the back of the head or through a small hole in each ear, is pretty."

> Darwin. *Journal of the Researches into the Natural History and Geology of the Countries visited during the Voyage round the World of H.M.S. Beagle under the command of Captain Fitz Roy, R.N.* (London Edition, 1901), p. 409.

3. *Descent of Man.*

4. Book V, 32.

5. *Politics* II, 6 & 7.

6. "The strange loves, of which the ancient poets' elegies are full, and which surprised us so

much and which we could not believe, are however possible and probable. In the translations we have made of them, we have substituted women's names for those originally there. Juventius was changed to Juventia, and Alexis to Xantha. The beautiful boys became beautiful women; so we recomposed the monstrous seraglio of Catullus, Tibullus, Martial and the gentle Virgil. It was a worthy occupation, which only proved how little we had understood the genius of antiquity."

> Gautier, *Mademoiselle de Maupin,* vol II,
> chap IX, pp. 13 and 14 (first edition).

7. Gérard de Nerval tells of two "seductive dancing girls," whom he saw performing in the most beautiful café of the Mousky in Egypt—whom he describes to us as "exceedingly beautiful, of proud bearing, with Arabic eyes brightened with kohl and with cheeks full and delicate"—at the moment when he "was preparing to place some gold coins on their foreheads, according to the finest traditions of the Middle East"—he noticed that the beautiful dancing girls were young boys, who at least deserved to have "a few pesetas thrown to them."

> *Voyages en Orient,* I, 140–41.

FOURTH DIALOGUE

1. It is interesting to quote here Napoleon's words: "Woman is given to man for the purpose of bearing him children. But one woman could not be sufficient for this purpose; she cannot be his wife when she is suckling; she cannot be his wife when she is sick; she ceases to be his wife when she can no longer give him children. The man who is not stopped by age or any of these inconveniences should therefore have several wives."

Mémorial (June, 1816).

2. Not always. It is fair to mention here Herder's discerning appreciation in his *Ideas on the Philosophy of History.*

3. So that one is tempted to agree with Nietzsche (when he is speaking of war and slavery): "No

one will be able to escape these conclusions, if he has honestly sought the causes of the perfection attained by Greek art, and by Greek art only." (Quoted by Halévy.)

4. cf. the passages from Pascal and Montaigne— and the account of the death of Epaminondas.

5. "The *Iliad*, therefore, has for its whole subject the passion of Achilles—that ardent energy or ΜΗΝΙΣ of the hero, which displayed itself first as anger against Agamemnon and afterwards as love for the lost Patroclus. The truth of this was perceived by one of the greatest poets and profoundest critics of the modern world, Dante. When Dante, in the Inferno wished to describe Achilles, he wrote, with characteristic brevity:

Achille,
Che per amore al fine combatteo.

Achilles,
Who at the last was brought to fight by love.

In this pregnant sentence Dante sounded the whole depth of the *Iliad*. The wrath of Achilles

212

against Agamemnon, which prevented him at first from fighting; the love of Achilles, passing the love of women, for Patroclus, which induced him to forego his anger and to fight at last—these are the two poles on which the *Iliad* turns."

J. A. Symonds, *Studies of the Greek Poets* (Harper and Brothers, Publishers, 1879), I, 95.

6. "Happy are those who love, when they are loved in return," said Bion in his eighth Idyll. Then he gave three examples of happy loves: Theseus and Pirithoüs, Orestes and Pylades, Achilles and Patroclus.

7. *Esprit des Lois* (*The Spirit of Laws*), IV, chap. 6, p. 154. Edition Garnier.

8. "He that opposes his own judgement against the current of the times ought to be backed with unanswerable truth, and he that has truth on his side is a fool as well as a coward, if he is afraid to

own it, because of the multitude of other men's opinions. 'Tis hard for a man to say, all the world is mistaken, but himself. But if it be so, who can help it?" Daniel Defoe (quoted by Taine in *Literature Anglaise*, IV, 87).

9. "Besides these public causes [of unhappiness], he had a private one, his excessive fondness for the son [of Spithridates], which touched him to the quick, though he endeavored to master it, and, especially in the presence of the boy, to suppress all appearance of it; so much so that when Megabates, for that was his name, came once to receive a kiss from him, he declined it. At which when the young boy blushed and drew back, and afterwards saluted him at a more reserved distance, Agesilaus soon repenting his coldness, and changing his mind, pretended to wonder why he did not salute him with the same familiarity as formerly. His friends about him answered, 'You are in fault, who would not accept the kiss of the boy, but turned away in alarm; he would come to you again, if you would have the courage to let him do so.' Upon this Agesilaus paused a while, and at length answered, 'You need not encourage him to do it; I think I had rather be master

of myself in that refusal, than see all things that are
now before my eyes turned into gold.' Thus he de-
meaned himself to Megabates when present, but he
had so great a passion for him in his absence, that it
may be questioned whether, if the boy had returned
again, all the courage he had would have sustained
him in such another refusal."

Plutarch's *Life of Agesilaus.*
From the translation called Dryden's,
corrected and revised by A. H. Clough.
Vol. IV, 13.

10. "The Persians, taught by the Greeks, have
learnt to sleep with boys."
Herodotus, I, 135.

11. *Atheneus*, XIII, 81. "Sophocles loved boys,
as much as Euripides loved women."
See also *Atheneus*, Chap. LXXXII

12. "Their lovers and favorers, too, had a share
in the young boy's honor or disgrace; and there goes

a story that one of them was fined by the magistrates, because the lad whom he loved cried out effeminately as he was fighting . . . they all (the lovers) conspired to render the object of their affection as accomplished as possible."

> Plutarch's *Life of Lycurgus*
> From the translation called Dryden's, corrected and revised by A. H. Clough.

13. The degree to which public opinion allows itself to be influenced in this connection, even to the point of flouting justice, is clearly shown by this article in *Le Matin* (7 August, 1909) following the Renard affair: "The Moral of a Trial" . . . "No defendant, for many years, has had so great an element of doubt in his favor as Renard when he appeared before the Seine Court of Assizes. The jury, however, did not hesitate and sentenced him to hard labor. Before the Versailles Court of Assizes, the element of doubt had increased even farther; but the Versailles jury condemned him without mercy. Before the Court of Appeal, there was a serious chance of the appeal being allowed; but it was instantly rejected. And public opinion—with the few rare excep-

tions that one would expect—was always on the side of the juries and magistrates . . . Why? Because it was proved that Renard, *while not guilty of murder,* was an odious, repugnant monster. Because the public had formed the opinion that Renard, though innocent of Mme. Renard's murder, belonged to that group of creatures, which society casts out and sends to stagnate in Guiana," etc.

14. See, in particular, Fielding, *Amelia* III, Chapters 3 & 4.

15. "Does any more delicate and noble sentiment exist than the friendship, at once passionate and shy, of one boy for another. The one who loves dares not express his affection by a caress, a look or a word. It is a clear-sighted tenderness, which suffers at the slightest fault of the one who is loved; it is made up of admiration, selflessness, pride, humility and serene happiness."

Jacobsen, *Nils Lyhne*, p. 69.

16. "Lubricity and physical ardor have little or nothing in common with love."

> Louise Labé, *Débat de folie et d'amour*, Discours III

APPENDICES

1. *L'amour qui n'ose pas dire son nom.* (The love that dares not tell its name.)

2. On the other hand when speaking of Balzac, you seem to have ignored his extraordinary *Vautrin*, the drama which the censor abruptly stopped in 1840. In this, Balzac presented a Jacques Collin more revealing and unmasked than in *Père Goriot* or *Lost Illusions*.

3. Quotations are from the Carlyle-Wicksteed translation, Modern Library.

218